DURHAM CATHEDRAL
Artists & Images

DURHAM CATHEDRAL
Artists & Images

Durham Cathedral as a Visual Image

An exhibition to celebrate the 900th anniversary
of Durham Cathedral

31st July - 3rd October 1993

Durham Art Gallery
Aykley Heads
Durham

Arts, Libraries and Museums Department
Durham County Council

Front Cover:
George Fennel Robson (1788-1833), *Durham Cathedral from Prebends' Bridge*. (Detail)
The Bowes Museum, Durham County Council (Cat. C.4)

Text by Patricia R. Andrew

Exhibition Organiser: Patricia R. Andrew
Project Assistant: Suzanne L. Robinson
Catalogue Design: David Boyes

Printed Durham County Council Print Services

ISBN 0 9520836 0 4

© Arts, Libraries and Museums Department
   Durham County Council, 1993

CONTENTS

Acknowledgments and thanks are due to all our lenders (see page 72) and to the following:

The Dean and Chapter of Durham; University of Durham Colleges ; The National Trust; The Royal Library, Windsor Castle ; Aberdeen Art Gallery and Museum; The Bodleian Library, Oxford; National Museum of Wales, Cardiff; P & O Containers Ltd.; The Tate Gallery, London; Whitworth Art Gallery, University of Manchester.

Individual thanks are due to: Rosemary Allen, Mrs. Anneliese Arnold, Alan Bowman, Sylvia Brand, Christina Bridgwater, Dr. Richard Brigstock, Julian Brown, Wing Commander A.E. Cartmell, Michael Chase, Canon R. Coppin, Ian Curry, The Rt. Rev. Lord Bishop of Durham, Mr.F.Gibbs, Frank Graham, Canon Bill Hall, Marshall Hall, The Rt. Hon. the Viscount Hampden DL, Gillian Jason, Tom Lamb, Caroline Mason, Roger Norris, Dr. Douglas Pocock, Miss Beth Rainey, Robert Raymond, Michael Richardson, Dr. Fiona Robertson, Fred Robinson, Frank Salmon, Mike Smith, Hugh Stevenson, Wendy Stevenson, Naomi Tarrant, Mr. P. Trigg, Maria Waller and Stephen Wildman.

Particular thanks are due to Suzanne Robinson, Project Assistant for the Exhibition; David Boyes, who designed the Catalogue; and all the staff of Durham Art Gallery .

Patricia R. Andrew

CHAIRMAN'S INTRODUCTION

This Catalogue has been produced to accompany the exhibition mounted by Durham Art Gallery to celebrate the 900th anniversary of Durham Cathedral.

This major project and its events programme would not have been possible without resources additional to the Gallery's normal funding; in this anniversary year the County Council has been pleased to provide special funding for these important celebrations.

Durham Cathedral is the focal point of the County - as the historic centre of worship, the symbol of its proud history and its present identity. I do hope that all our visitors enjoy the exhibition and revisit the Cathedral with a renewed interest.

Cllr. Stella Robinson

Chairman, Arts, Libraries and Museums Committee
Durham County Council

Hilary Paynter, *Durham* (1980), Cat. F. 29. (reproduced actual size)

INTRODUCTION

In preparing an exhibition on such a well recorded visual theme, one is overwhelmed by the sheer volume of material available. Rather than attempt to list all the artists who have depicted the Cathedral, it is easier to list those few who have not done so. Thus, the exhibition is inevitably a mere taste of what was produced in each period since the Cathedral's construction.

I have sought to discover exactly what material does exist by writing to a wide range of public collections in Britain and abroad. Images abound worldwide - from Connecticut to California, from Madrid to Wellington, New Zealand (one very large painting, Ralph Hedley's *Seeking Sanctuary*, Cat. I.1, has been brought from Australia by the generosity of P & O Containers). The collated information will be retained as a research resource. From it, I have selected a mixture of paintings not seen before in public exhibitions, together with a few well-known images. A wide range of media and sizes is represented, though the largest and smallest pictures I have found - the mural in Durham's County Hall (seven metres/twenty-three feet in length) and the picture in the Royal Dolls' House at Windsor Castle (approximately three by five centimetres/one by two inches) - are to be visited 'in situ' rather than seen here!

One aspect has struck me repeatedly in the course of my research. Although the Cathedral is a religious building, pictorial convention and social attitudes have dictated that it be represented, until recent times, as an architectural, picturesque or symbolic image. It is only since the 1980s that a new generation of artists has sought to make a personal response on a spiritual or emotional level.

The theme of the exhibition is the visual response to the structure of the Cathedral. It is such a broad subject in itself that I have not attempted to include the work of artists or craftsmen such as stonemasons and stained glass designers who have contributed to the structure or decoration of the building itself. Also, I have not sought to cover the numerous depictions of St. Cuthbert, St. Bede or the Bishops of the Cathedral. The building itself, as an inspiration to artists, is the subject of the exhibition.

Patricia R. Andrew

May 1993

Daniel King, *Durham Cathedral* (1656), *West Prospect*, Cat. A.4.

EARLY IMAGES: THE TOPOGRAPHERS

Early images of Durham Cathedral are difficult to date. The precise dates of the artists themselves are often unknown, and they frequently chose to depict the building in a time which was already the historic past.

Daniel King (1610 - c1664) produced his workmanlike etchings in the mid 1660s. Like most prints produced up to the 1860s, they were made as illustration for books, in this case King's own *The Cathedral and Conventual Churches of England and Wales* of 1656, and Dugdale's *Monasticon Anglicanum* of 1655 and 1682.

One image, the *South View* (Cat. A.3.) appears to be confused in design with another building - King seems to have realised this for he left it out of his own publication, though it was

Samuel Buck, *Durham Cathedral* (early 18th century), Cat. A.9.

included in various editions of the *Monasticon*. His prints show the lead-covered spires or 'great broaches' of the Western towers, taken down in the 1650s just a few years earlier. There are a few inaccuracies in other details - he may well have worked from the drawings of other artists and perhaps never visited Durham himself. He completely omits the surroundings of the Cathedral, taking no opportunity to display the drama of its setting.

The oil painting by Samuel Buck (1696 -1779) was produced early in

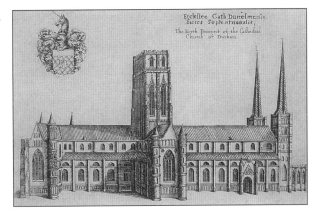

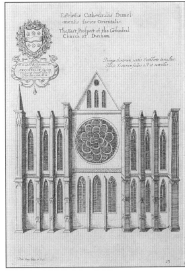

Daniel King, *Durham Cathedral* (1656)
(centre) *North Prospect*, Cat.A.1.
(right) *East Prospect*, Cat.A.2.

the next century but also shows the pre-1660s towers, now history rather than common memory (Cat. A.9). The Cathedral stands massive but alone, with no indication of whether it is on a crag, a gentle slope or a flat plain. Indeed, several of the early engravers, copying the work of other draughtsmen, show it sitting on a flat surface which spreads out around in all directions for some distance (see p.29).

(?) Samuel Buck, *Durham Cathedral and Castle, with Bishop's Barge*, Cat. A.10.

Samuel Buck and his brother Nathaniel worked principally as engravers, hence the schematic approach. But another large oil painting, possibly also by Samuel Buck, shows a more scenic view looking up from the River Wear, with the stylish Bishop John Cosin (Bishop from 1660 to 1672) in his Venetian-style gondola (Cat.A.10).

Panoramic pictures of the City appear from the early 1770s, influenced by continental artists such as Wenceslaus Hollar and the British artist Francis Place. One enormous oil painting in grisaille (ie. monochrome), by an anonymous artist working around 1700, is fascinating both in its detail and in its style - it could almost be mistaken for a consciously 'naive' painting of the twentieth century (Cat.A.11).

Large numbers of panoramic 'Views' of cities were produced as prints in the early 1700s. Later in the century landscape painting diverged into the 'picturesque' on the one hand, and the more refined and

detailed accuracy of topographical prints on the other. Three pictures -*The South-West Prospect of the City of Durham* published in the *Universal Magazine* in 1749, *The Perspective View* published in the *Complete English Traveller*, and Forster and Mynde's four perspective prints of the 1750s - all serve to show how small the City still was, how rural the setting, and how much more of a surprise the sheer scale of the

Anonymous artist, *Panorama of Durham City and Environs*, (c.1700), Cat.A.11.

Anonymous artist, *Perspective View* (before1771), Cat.A.6.

Cathedral would have been to the traveller of those days (Cats. A.5, A.6, A.7). The few early oil paintings were probably taken from such prints (see illustration bottom of next page).

John Clerk of Eldin (1728-1812) was unusual in his approach as a fine artist rather than an illustrator. His etching of *Durham Cathedral* made in 1774-5 (Cat. A.8) is also rare in the context of his own work as he produced few views of any non-Scottish subjects. He was taught by his friend the artist Paul Sandby, whom he met in the late 1770s, and was also influenced by the work of European etchers. Clerk produced over 110 etchings from about 1770 to 1778. He has left details of his methods and of his frustrations with the fiddly nature of the medium. In a letter to Sandby he relates being 'driven to make use of spectacles' by the reverse nature of the method, 'the bright trace of the point upon ye black grounded copper, compared with the black inky lines upon white paper - to get the better of this difficulty I have been led to make many trials which has produced so very many diminuitive plates as unfortunately I have made '. His *Durham Cathedral* is in fact one of his larger prints, the only one made from several sketches of Durham. Proportions have changed between sketch and print, and the City is portrayed almost from imagination.

Samuel Hieronymus Grimm (1733-1794) is one of the greatest eighteenth-century topographers. He was born and

Photograph of the version in the National Gallery of Scotland, Edinburgh

John Clerk of Eldin, *Durham Cathedral* (1774-5), Cat. A. 8.

Samuel Hieronymous Grimm, *North View up the River Wear at Durham* (late 18th century), Cat.A.12.

trained in Switzerland, working later in France. He arrived in England in 1768, quickly becoming established in the art world and exhibiting regularly at the Royal Academy from 1769. He produced numerous drawings for individual patrons and his work was much sought after. Sir Richard Kaye (1736-1809), Prebend of Durham and Southwell, was one of his major patrons and Grimm undertook a northern sketching tour for him in the 1770s, recording over a hundred sites.

Grimm is one of the first topographers to bother with people in the landscape; they are no mere decoration, being actively engaged in work or even pursuits such as swimming (Cat A.17). Several Durham views are still held in the north of England, but Sir Richard Kaye bequeathed most of his

collection of Grimm's sketches to the British Museum; they are now part of the British Library's collection, filling twelve stout volumes. The Durham sketches include distant views from 'Akely Head' and 'Chincliff', City viewpoints such as *The North View* (Cat. A.12, illustrated above), details of the Dean's kitchen (Cat. A.16), services in the Cathedral (Cat. A.18.) and the carving of the Dun Cow and a nearby thorn tree (Cats. A.14, A.15). The 'Dun Cow' shows

Anonymous Artist, *View of Durham*, mid-18th century, 44.3 x 80.7cms, Coll. The Rt. Hon. Viscount Hampden, Glynde Place, Sussex (not in exhibition)

milkmaids and a cow, illustrating the legend that a girl and her dun cow indicated to St. Cuthbert's followers the exact site of 'Dunholm' as the final resting place of the Saint's coffin.

THE PICTURESQUE

By the mid-eighteenth century the theories of the Picturesque, the Sublime and the Beautiful had taken hold on the popular imagination. While printmakers continued to work in a precise, detailed manner for book illustrations and collections, artists working in oil or the new (portable) medium of watercolour freed themselves from the formality of mere depiction and turned to compositions of the Sublime, Romanticism and the Picturesque.

Edward Dayes (1763-1804) bridges the two traditions, working as a miniaturist and topographer but also creating a

Edward Dayes, *Durham Cathedral from beneath an Arch of Ralph Flambard's Bridge: Moonlight* (1797), Cat.B.3.

The Visitors of the Ashmolean Museum, Oxford

new atmosphere in his detailed watercolours (and teaching the great watercolourist Thomas Girtin - see next page). His tiny watercolour entitled *Durham Cathedral from beneath an Arch of Ralph Flambard's Bridge, Moonlight* of 1797 (Cat. B.3) shows a dramatic view glimpsed through the peephole of the bridge's elegant curve. Dayes produced a number of Durham views in the 1790s, some engraved for books (see p.29), and generally seems to have favoured a viewpoint looking up to the Cathedral to heighten the dramatic effect and to personalise the experience. In his *Instructions for Drawing and Coloring Landscapes*, published in 1805, he bemoaned the 'common prejudice among mankind ... that to take a view the person must get on a hill: this will always produce what is called a bird's-eye view, and will never look well... It

William Daniell, *Durham Cathedral* (1805), Cat.B.4.

is really surprising how many of the old views were manufactured, when it is considered that balloons were not in use...'.

William Daniell (1769-1837) was a well-travelled artist whose compositions were far more panoramic. He visited the City in 1803, showing three Durham subjects at the Royal Academy exhibition in 1806 and two at the British Institution the following year. His best known version of *Durham Cathedral* is now in the collection of the Victoria and Albert Museum, London

Edward Blore, *Durham Cathedral: West Front* , Cat.B.1.

(Cat. B.4). It has a dramatic play of light and shadow, with the tops of the towers catching the last of the evening light. The central placing of Framwellgate Bridge opens up a long-distance view which other artists rarely portray; the tranquillity of the river adds to a powerful monumentality with a sombre, restricted colour range (now somewhat faded). Despite the simplicity of the effect, however, the picture actually has more people in it than many other versions of the same view.

The view of John Pearson (1777-c1813) is a more workaday affair, with a homely mill under a gentler, bushy hill up to the Cathedral (Cat. B.5).

Edward Blore (1789-1879) continues the topographical tradition, with detailed watercolours of great charm and dignity. His careful studies of the Cathedral's architecture, now in the British Library, were engraved in 1823 and included in Surtees' *The History and Antiquities of the County Palatine of Durham* (vol. IV, published 1840). He took immense pains with detailing and with shadow: two versions of the *Choir* exist, a pencil sketch and the finished watercolour (Cats. B.1, B.2).

Thomas Girtin, *Durham Cathedral* (1796-99), Cat.B.6.

Thomas Girtin, *Durham Cathedral* (1799), Whitworth Art Gallery, University of Manchester (not in exhibition)

While Turner is reckoned nowadays to be Britain's greatest landscape painter, he is one of a trio of eminent British watercolourists, the other two being the short-lived Thomas Girtin (1775-1802) and John Sell Cotman (1782-1842). All three visited Durham, producing very different, dramatic and picturesque impressions of the scene.

London-born, Girtin first came to the North of England in the 1790s, and his Durham work dates from between 1795 and 1799. He painted several views of the City and Cathedral: one, in the Laing Art Gallery, Newcastle upon Tyne, is clearly in the style of his teacher Edward Dayes (see p.15). His work was admired by Turner - 'If Girtin had lived, I should have starved' is Turner's apocryphal comment. Girtin had great skill in rendering the structure of buildings in simple, direct dabs of colour and showing every last detail without losing the overall 'picturesque' composition to the precision of a draughtsman. His view from the south (Cat. B.6.) shows a rather rural Cathedral; a grander composition including the strong horizontal lines of Framwellgate Bridge shows it as a central part of the rocky city.

J.M.W. Turner, *Durham Cathedral* (c.1799), Cat. B.7.

There are several other views in British art galleries, including the Whitworth Art Gallery, University of Manchester (illustrated p. 16), Birmingham Museum and Art Gallery, and the Victoria and Albert Museum, London.

The work of Joseph Mallord William Turner (1775-1851) covers the full range of interpretation from careful topographical delineation to a romantic, visionary style in which the depiction of buildings becomes of less importance than the atmosphere created. Until 1796 he worked entirely in the topographical tradition but then took to a wider style.

Turner's earliest studies of Durham are in the Tate Gallery's 'Tweed and Lakes' Sketchbook made in the summer of 1797. One of these was enlarged about 1799 to make the version now belonging to the Royal Academy of Arts, painted as a gift for the artist John Hoppner and later presented by him to the Royal Academy (Cat. B.7). The pencil sketch is extremely precise and shows his training as an architectural draughtsman, but the golden flow of the finished piece has an ethereal quality transcending mere topography. (Another example is the National Gallery of Scotland's *Durham Cathedral*, worked up many years later with less topographical accuracy - a print taken from it is discussed p. 30).

Some of his watercolour sketches, however, are so loose as to be mere splashes and blobs of colour. For Turner, watercolour was a medium of exploration and he showed few examples as finished pictures.

J.M.W. Turner, *Durham Cathedral*, 1797-8, Tate Gallery, London (not in exhibition)

J.M.W. Turner, *Durham Cathedral* from 'Tweed and Lakes' sketchbook, Tate Gallery, London (not in exhibition)

J.M.W. Turner, *Durham Cathedral* from sketchbook, Tate Gallery, London (not in exhibition)

The diarist Joseph Farington visited his studio in 1798, and was shown 'two books filled with studies from Nature - several of them tinted on the Spot, which He found, He said, were much the most valuable to him ... studies at Doncaster, - York, - Durham, - Melrose ...' (24 October 1798). The following year Farington also noted that Turner had 'no systematic process for making drawings ... By washing and occasionally rubbing out, he at last expresses in some degree the idea in his mind' (July 1799).

Turner was as interested in the interior of the Cathedral as its exterior. The large *Durham Cathedral Looking East along the South Aisle* of 1797-8 (illus. p.17) in pencil, watercolour, and bodycolour is based on a sketchbook drawing. The arches sweep up into the gloom while dramatic shafts of sunlight pierce the darkness. There is artistic licence here: the screen across the entrance to the choir is omitted (though present in his original sketch).

John Sell Cotman (1782-1842) was not so much attracted to Durham as chivvied into visiting it. He made sketching tours of Wales in 1800 and Yorkshire in 1803; during another Yorkshire visit of 1805 he was urged to 'storm Durham' by his Yorkshire hostess Mrs. Cholmeley; 'but seriously what have I to do with Durham? ... No and besides I have not time for Durham' he wrote to her son in August. But he arrived a week later and found it 'a delightfully situated City' and described it to the first owner of his *Durham Cathedral* (Cat. B.9) as 'magnificent tho' not so fine as York'. His dramatic view looking up to the Cathedral is a careful composition of limpid flat areas of watercolour washes in contrasting light and shade, with simplified blocks of heavy architecture. The broader *View of Durham from the North-West* (Cat. B.8) is a delicate essay in outline and silhouette, the dark central tower dominating the scene. A further schematic view is taken

John Sell Cotman, *Durham Cathedral* (1806), Cat. B.9.

from below Framwellgate Bridge, reducing everything to blocks of light and shade (Norwich Castle Museum).

John Glover (1767-1849) was a more predictable artist of the Picturesque. He worked in both oil and watercolour, becoming a prolific exhibitor at the Old Water-Colour Society of which he was a founder member and President. A restless individual, he emigrated to Australia in 1830 and became one of the most important shaping influences on the art of the European settlers. The oil painting attributed to Glover in the Cathedral's own collection (Cat.B.10) is a very idealised scene in the style of continental seventeenth-century painters and the English landscape artist Richard Wilson. A Durham sketchbook by Glover is held in the Laing Art

John Sell Cotman, *View of Durham from the North West*, Cat. B.8.

Gallery, Newcastle upon Tyne, and a large-scale watercolour of a similar Durham composition was sold recently at Sotheby's.

Many other artists came here on their 'picturesque' tours; works by Thomas Hearne (1744-1817) and Edward Edwards (1738-1806) have been shown at Durham Art Gallery in previous exhibitions. Francis Towne (1740-1816) painted a long, wide, horizontal view from Prebends' Bridge in 1811 (sold in London in 1991). Highly trained amateurs abounded as watercolour painting became a proper accomplishment of young ladies and gentlemen. The Laing Art Gallery in Newcastle upon Tyne holds a typical landscape view by Cecilia Priscilla Cooke in pencil, ink and watercolour; the National Museum of Scotland has a view in embroidered silk. Both of these, and many other amateur examples, may have been taken from prints.

John Glover, *Durham Cathedral*, Cat. B.10.

Felix Mendelssohn-Bartholdy, *Durham Cathedral, 24th July 1829*, Bodleian Library, University of Oxford (not in exhibition)

Felix Mendelssohn-Bartholdy, *Durham Cathedral* (1829), Cat. B.11.

In 1829, the composer Felix Mendelssohn-Bartholdy (1809-1847) set out for several years of foreign travel. In April of that year he accepted an invitation to London from an acquaintance, Karl Klingemann, who lived in England as a diplomat and who introduced him into London salons and social life.

He travelled to Edinburgh with Klingemann in June, stopping at York and Durham en route. The resulting painting is now in the Mendelssohn Archive of the Staatsbibliothek Preussicher Kulturbesitz in Berlin. Due to the architectural distortions in the painting, it has often been assumed that it was painted entirely from memory. In fact, whenever the two travellers came to a good view they wished to record, Mendelssohn drew it in his sketchbook and Klingemann composed a short poem which he wrote underneath. The drawings are still in Mendelssohn's Scottish Sketchbook held in the Bodleian Library, University of Oxford. Two pencil sketches were made of Durham Cathedral from across the river: one from which the painting was later taken and one from another vantage point on the same path, dated 24th July. These drawings already show slight oddities in the recording of perspective and design - a feature which was exaggerated later when Mendelssohn turned the Cathedral into a white 'Castle on the Rhine'(B.11).

C

THE GRAND VIEW

During the course of the eighteenth century, landscape painting fought to be recognised as a subject of equal worth with portrait and history painting. By the nineteenth century it had come into its own as the most typical subject matter for both oil and watercolour painting.

George Fennel Robson (1788-1833) is *the* Durham painter. He produced more views of Durham and its Cathedral than any other artist before or since - possibly as many as all other artists put together. He was born in Durham, the son of a wine merchant,

The Visitors of the Ashmolean Museum, Oxford

George Fennel Robson, *Durham Cathedral and Castle from across the River*, Cat. C.3.

was taught by a local man called Harle, and left for London when he surpassed his master's abilities. He began to exhibit at the Royal Academy in 1807 and the following year published a print of Durham which was so successful that it made his name and brought him enough income to travel to Scotland. From then on his favourite themes were Durham City and Scottish mountain scenery. He produced vast numbers of pictures for public show, becoming a leading member of the Old Water-Colour Society and its President in 1820 (he exhibited nearly five hundred works there between 1821 and 1833, with eighty-nine views of Durham alone). Many small-scale works were expressly produced for engravings, to be included in books such as John Britton's *Picturesque Views of the Cities of England* .

Between 1826 and 1829 he embarked on a very different project for his patron Mrs. George Haldimand, the wife of a London financier, forming a representative collection of a hundred of the best watercolours of the period - it was kept as one collection until sold at Christie's in 1861 and again in 1980, when it was dispersed. This collection also included a *Durham Cathedral* by Frederick Nash (see p.32).

Robson died in 1833 on his way from London to Durham, taken ill on the James Watt steamboat on its way to

George Fennel Robson, *Durham* , Cat. C.5.

Stockton-on-Tees. He is buried in the churchyard of St. Mary-le-Bow Church in Durham.

Robson's views of *Durham Cathedral* have found their way into numerous collections, including most north-east galleries and private collections and almost every other major British art gallery, from Penrhyn Castle in Wales (National Trust) to Norwich Castle Museum (Norfolk Museums Service), from Eton College to the Victoria and Albert Museum. His work cannot be said to be greatly innovative but it is of a high standard. Influenced by the landscape painter John Varley, it shows an immense flair, some very original viewpoints, sensitive handling of aerial perspective and a clever habit of slightly distorting scale and perspective to make a scene appear grander than it actually is.

The version in the Ashmolean Museum, Oxford (Cat. C.3) shows the Cathedral towers narrowed and elongated, and a silhouetted distant view of other buildings to the left which makes the whole City seem fortress-like, across the 'moat' of the Wear from the surrounding countryside. The 'fairy-tale' castle effect is taken further in another view now in the Victoria and Albert Museum (Cat. C.2) where even more elongated stone structures rise beyond the verdant fields, with a skirt of smoky chimneys (from hindsight this picture is interesting as a view from Flass Vale before the railway viaduct was built). It is not perhaps a coincidence that Robson was much taken with the romanticism of Sir Walter Scott's novels. Robson could, however, paint Durham in more prosaic terms: the version in the Bowes Museum (Cat. C.4, front cover) shows stonemasons at work on Prebends' Bridge (completed in 1778, before Robson was born). Even these mundane activities do not detract from the customary air of tranquillity, peace and warmth.

Robson's work comes in a great variety of sizes - grand watercolours with opaque bodycolour, with the status of oils complete with gilt frames, to tiny, delicate watercolours made for engravers to work from. It is remarkable how similar the compositions and style remain despite such different formats.

John Dobbin, *Durham* (1854), Cat. C.6.

John Dobbin is another regional artist, born in Darlington in 1815. He moved to London in his mid-twenties, exhibiting his work in the 1840s and 1850s. Most of his grand landscapes feature historic or ecclesiastical buildings, though he is best known for his picture of the opening of the Stockton and Darlington railway in 1825. His view of *Durham* in 1854 (Cat. C.6) is a good example of a grandiose mid-century painting.

Many other artists visited Durham during this period. The great Scottish painter Alexander Nasmyth (1758-1840) produced a monumental view of Durham from the east in 1809. Thomas Shotter Boys (1803-1874), produced several views which are similar to Robson's in composition though less grandiose in style. David Roberts (1796-1864) came on a rather rainy sketching tour in 1836, which resulted in a painting now in Leeds City Art Galleries.

John Wilson Carmichael, *Durham* (?1841), Cat. C.7.

Among a group of successful north-east artists of the mid-nineteenth century, John Wilson Carmichael (1799-1868) stands out for his compositions of landscapes and seascapes. He produced quite a number of large, detailed paintings of Durham in which he skillfully maintained the Cathedral as the prime area of interest while delineating the City and surrounding villages and countryside in great detail . Two pictures from Observatory Hill to the south-west (Cats. C.7, C.9) are typical of his work. His use of shadow enables him to highlight features without losing the detail of subordinate elements.

Carmichael came from Newcastle, went to sea at an early age and was best known as a marine artist. Although he spent almost twenty years in London he came back to Scarborough in 1864 and continued to paint his native north east. Tyne and Wear Museums Service holds the largest collection of his work, with over five hundred drawings including a pencil drawing and engraving similar to these views (a lithograph by Hawkins is included in this exhibition, Cat. E.20).

Thomas Miles Richardson Junior (1813-1890) produced panoramic watercolours in a style similar to Carmichael's, including a large *City of Durham* of 1860, sold in 1992 in a Newcastle auction.

Edmund Hastings (1781-1861) applied the grandiose vision to the interior of the Cathedral. But gone is the mystery and dimly-lit atmosphere of the picturesque artists and engravers - this is a truly 'official' picture of the pomp and majesty of local dignitaries assembled in the *Cathedral Choir, Assize Sunday, 1835* (Cat. C.8). The architecture is rendered carefully but blandly, an essay in symmetry and size (a large preliminary watercolour of the scene without the figures hangs in the Dean and Chapter Office). Very few artists ever took a central view down the nave but

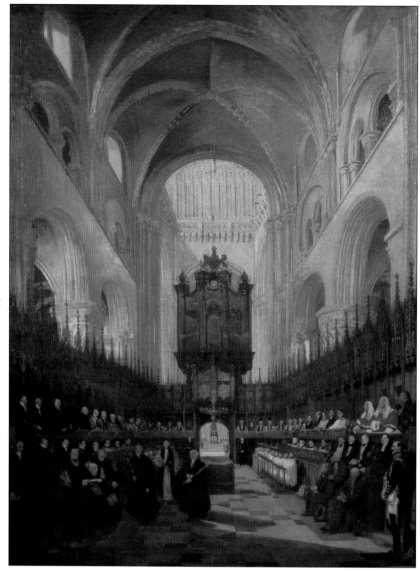

Edmund Hastings, *Cathedral Choir, Assize Sunday 1835*, Cat. C.8.

here we see all the way, from a slightly raised position on the altar steps through the choir and the nave to the font. Figures are placed carefully on the way to give a sense of scale. The organ screen which features so prominently was built between 1683 and 1686 by (Father) Bernard Smith. It was taken down just twelve years later to open up the vista from the nave to the choir.

Hastings produced numerous other paintings of Durham, including an impressive view from South Street of around 1810 (now in a private Durham collection). Some of his work, however, could be delightfully informal (Cats. F.2, F.3, p.35).

ARCHITECTS AND ANTIQUARIANS 1800-1950

John Carter (1748-1817) was an indefatigable draughtsman - over twenty volumes of his 'Sketches relating to the Antiquities of this Kingdom' are now held in the British Library. From 1780 he worked for the Society of Antiquaries, producing architectural drawings; he also wrote on Gothic architecture. Carter specialised in faithful recordings of ancient buildings from an architect's point of view. There is no crumbling stonework or evidence of decay - buildings are depicted as they were constructed, pristine and complete. His plans and elevations of Durham Cathedral were published in 1801 as *Some Account of the Cathedral Church of Durham...* and Plate IV, *Elevation of the North Front*, is shown here (Cat. D.2).

Carter was a nervous, eccentric individual, ill-suited to the architectural practice of his early career, and he turned to making a living drawing mediaeval antiquities, publishing a series on Cathedrals between 1795 and 1813. He inveighed against the thoughtless 'restoration' then in vogue, which often involved the destruction of large parts of ecclesiastical buildings. In Durham and elsewhere, he particularly opposed the activities of architect James Wyatt (see p.26).

Robert William Billings (1813-1874) was probably, however, the greatest architectural 'recorder' of Durham Cathedral. His work combines the precision and detail of the finest professional draughtsmanship with a lively sense of humanity and even humour. What stands out most in his prints

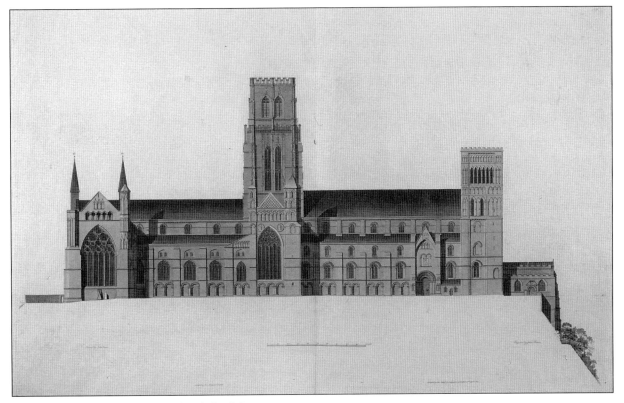

John Carter, *Elevation of the North Front* (1801), Cat. D.2.

John Saddler after R. W. Billings, *Durham Cathedral. Elevation of the West Front* (1843), Cat. D.4.

John Saddler after R. W. Billings, *Durham Cathedral. Chapel of the Nine Altars, Groining, South End* Cat. D.7.

is a sense of curiosity; the people in his drawings are there not simply to give scale to a scene or to fill in the foreground, they are usually *doing* something - lowering plumblines to measure the building, pointing out bits of architecture to each other, drawing a landscape, or simply getting on with a day's work (Cats. D.4-9).

Billings trained under the eminent topographer John Britton and went on to produce numerous series of drawings and publications on historic buildings, churches and cathedrals. His book on Durham Cathedral, *Architectural Illustrations and Description of the Cathedral Church at Durham*, appeared in 1843, to be followed by the *Illustrations of the Architectural Antiquities of the County of Durham* (including the Cathedral) in 1846. The beautifully-coloured watercolour drawings for the *Antiquities* survive, mounted into a specially bound copy of the publication held in the Library of the Royal Institute of British Architects.

Another architectural draughtsman, John Buckler (1770-1851) drew and etched a fine view of the Cathedral from an unusual north-east vantage point, publishing an engraved version of it dedicated to Bishop Shute Barrington (Cat.D.3). It was one of a series of engravings he produced of English Cathedrals and he was also noted for his architectural watercolours, delicate and detailed in style. A watercolour version of this print hangs in Durham Cathedral's Chapter Office.

John Saddler after R. W. Billings, *Durham Cathedral. Triforium of the Nave - North Side* (1842), Cat. D.8.

Various plans for altering and 'improving' the Cathedral have been made over the centuries, many of which have never come to fruition. The most radical and disastrous recommendations came from the architect James Wyatt, appointed consultant in 1794. A folio of his drawings is held by the Chapter

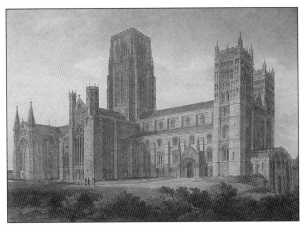

R. Reeve after John Buckler, *North West View of the Cathedral Church of Durham* (1809), Cat. D.3.

Library and includes two designs for the *East Front of the Nine Altars Chapel* (one illustrated here, Cat. D.1). He also proposed a spire, never built, which he drew in a set of watercolours (now held by the University of Manchester's School of Architecture, see illustration bottom of page). He is unfortunately best remembered as the architect who demolished the Chapter House; his proposal to demolish the Galilee Chapel was successfully resisted by public opinion, partly mobilised by the efforts of John Carter (see p.25).

Giles Gilbert Scott was one of the great Victorian church architects; he worked on Durham in the 1850s and 1860s. Like Wyatt, he too proposed a spire, in 1860 (shown next page, Cat. D.10), an open crown on flying buttresses supported by pinnacles, similar to that of the 15th-century corona of St. Nicholas, Newcastle (which he was later to restore). His plan was turned down but he heightened the pierced battlements and the square pinnacles surmounting the corner buttresses. He also designed the marble and alabaster choir screen, completed 1876, and the elaborately geometric marble choir floor, 1870-75.

James Wyatt, *Plans for Durham Cathedral: Elevation of the East End* (1795), Cat. D.1.

The Dean and Chapter Library holds many designs for alterations to the Cathedral's fabric, and reconstructions of the building as it used to be. T.D.Micklethwaite drew a detailed reconstruction of the

James Wyatt, *Design for a Spire, Durham Cathedral* (1795), (not in exhibition)

High Altar and Neville Screen as it existed before the Reformation; in 1885 T. Nicholls also produced a version of the Screen in its original form, with alabaster images, lost during the Reformation. Francis Bedford's *Bishop Hatfield's Tomb* of 1893 (Cat. D.12), reproduced in the magazine *The Builder*, well exhibits the precision and detailing so typical of Victorian antiquarians. Details of worn stone are recorded carefully; the artist's own signature intrudes within the border of the drawing to emphasise that he was there and that the picture is the result of personal study. Mark Thompson's *Bishop's Throne* is another highly-coloured version of the same style of illustration - a great delight taken in the detailing and 'picture-book' colouring (Cat.D.13). An anonymous photo-lithograph of *Durham*

Giles Gilbert Scott, *Design for a Spire, Durham Cathedral* (1859-1860),
Cat. D.10.

Mark Thompson, *The Bishop's Throne in Durham Cathedral* (1836), Cat. D.13.

Monastery before the Dissolution, a conjectural restoration 'chiefly from existing remains', was published in *The British Architect and Northern Engineer* in 1878. A reconstruction of Karileph's Church as it was in 1133, by an anonymous artist, was reproduced in *The Ecclesiologist* in 1862 (Cat. D. 11). The architect Sir Reginald Blomfield (1856-1942) made study drawings of the Cathedral in his sketchbooks (Cat. D.15). More recent is Sir Ninian Comper's design for a tester and candlesticks at St. Cuthbert's Shrine of 1947 (Cat. D.14.) which were constructed in 1949, with a few variations.

The interest in purely architectural investigation which began with Carter and Billings continues. Ian Curry, appointed Cathedral Architect in 1976, has examined the work of Durham Cathedral's previous architects in his generously titled *Sense and Sensitivity: Durham Cathedral and its Architects*, a lecture delivered in the Prior's Hall in 1985 and since published (Cat. D.16). He followed this with a detailed architectural study into *Aspects of the Anglo-Norman Design of Durham Cathedral*, 1986, with new plans and elevations (Cat. D.17). Like so many before him, he has 'become enthralled by all aspects of the building, and particularly by its design and construction'.

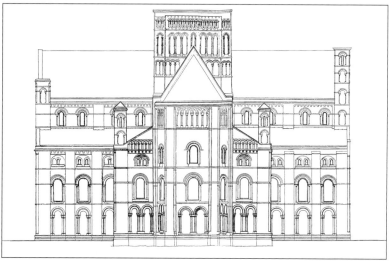

Ian Curry, *East Elevation with Apse (conjectural) and Transepts (existing)* (1986), Cat D.17.

PRINTMAKERS AND TRAVELLERS

The century from 1750 to 1850 was the printmaker's heyday. Though we now often buy 'genuine 100 year old prints', individually mounted and wrapped in cellophane, the vast majority of them were produced as book illustrations for the many publications of *Views* and *Cities* of Britain which enjoyed such popularity before photography.

Until this period many painters and printmakers of landscapes had been foreigners and the best work in Britain was undertaken by artists such as Hollar, Bok and Kip. But, as Edward Dayes (see p.15) wrote in 1805, 'the excellence of our artists has turned the balance of trade in our favor. For though we formerly imported vast quantities of prints, we now supply all Europe, and import very few...'.

The earliest book illustrations are small and rather schematic, and engravers often worked without reference to the Cathedral's setting. In Griffiths and Sparrow's example the weir is omitted (Cat. E.1). Thornton's Cathedral is like a doll's house, placed upon a flat floor with no surrounding buildings, or crags at the west end (Cat E.2). An engraving from a painting by the landscape artist Paul Sandby of 1780 (Cat. E.3) moves towards the new concept of the Picturesque. Two by Edward Dayes (Cats. E.4, E.5) are far more successful in their attempts to translate paintings to prints: the first (Cat. E.4) has a lively sky, and shows a carriage crossing Prebends' Bridge and punters on the river; the second shows the scaffolding on the south-west tower for the construction of the open parapets in 1786 (Cat. E.5), and smoke rising from chimneys. Like many prints, it also shows the Wear running in the wrong direction; printmakers had to engrave the scene on a metal plate in reverse, in order to produce an image the right way round.

From the 1830s steel took over from copper as the plate medium for engraved illustrations. This enabled engravers to produce finer lines, more detailing, and larger print runs as the plates stood up to more wear.

Several printmakers specialised in 'picturesque' views. John Le Keux was one of two brothers who worked mainly on line engravings, particularly in association with the publisher John Britton. A view engraved after a watercolour by the prolific

Sparrow after Moses Griffiths, *The Cathedral Church and Bridge of Durham* (1776), Cat. E.1.

(?Thomas) Thornton, *View of the Cathedral Church of Durham* (1786), Cat. E.2.

James Storer after Edward Dayes, *Durham* (1796), Cat E.4.

William Angus after Edward Dayes, *Durham* (1801), Cat. E.5.

John Le Keux after George Fennel Robson, *North East View of the City of Durham* (1828), Cat. E.9.

George Fennel Robson (see pp.21-22) was published in Britton's *Picturesque Antiquities of English Cities* in 1830 and dedicated to Archdeacon Prosser (Cat.E.9). Robson's grand oil paintings inspired grand engravings on a miniature scale: Edward Finden, and a partnership of Winkles and Taylor, produced amazing details using magnifying glasses and painstaking patience (Cats. E.10, E.11). Many of these engravers produced their own publications, such as Winkles' *Cathedral Church of Durham* published in Durham in 1842, and J. and H. Storer's *History and Antiquities of the Cathedral Church of Durham* (London, 1819).

William Miller after J. M. W. Turner, *Durham Cathedral*, Cat. E.16.

Two engravings of Durham Cathedral were made after Turner's work. The first is an interior engraved by Samuel Porter with an oblique view of the nave lit by shafts of light: it appeared in Warton's *Essays on Gothic Architecture* (2nd edition, 1802). The second, by William Miller, is dated 1836 (Cat. E.16). For this view of the Cathedral from Prebends' Bridge, produced for Charles Heath's *Picturesque Views in England and Wales*, Turner worked up a drawing into a watercolour some thirty years after he originally sketched it, transforming the Cathedral and river into a magical, fairy-tale scene with complete disregard for perspective and relative size. The watercolour is now in the National Gallery of Scotland.

Turner gave detailed instructions to his engravers and in a note, written on a 'proof' stage engraving on this scene he emphasised the importance of achieving a sense of mass and gradation - 'All the Bank is covered with Trees down to the River Edge. I want [illegible] large Trees to be made out. Excuse my saying, everything you try to make [?]

E. Young after T. Allom, *Interior of Durham Cathedral from the Nine Altars* (1835), Cat. E.14.

out by single line only, and that way too frequently done without Form has nothing characteristic of masses of light and shadow.' In fact, Turner is simply highlighting the problem faced by every engraver trying to reproduce a 'picturesque' landscape. His close

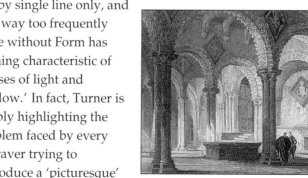

J. Redaway after T. Allom *The Galilee, West End of Durham Cathedral*, Cat. E.12.

William Brown, *Durham from the Upper Part of ClayPath*, (1809) Cat. E.7.

interest and supervision of the work of his engravers did, however, ensure plates of very high quality, as did his insistence on the use of copper plates rather than the more hard-wearing and economical steel.

Thomas Allom (1804-1872) was perhaps the most prolific supplier of drawings and paintings produced specifically for engravers to work on. He was trained as an architect and was quick and accurate in the rendering of detail while not ignoring the overall demands of artistic composition. He produced grand views from a

distance (such as Cat. E.13), interiors with 'Turneresque' shafts of light (Cat. E.14) and domestic town scenes such as the 'standard' view from below Framwellgate Bridge at the City's watering place, with washerwomen and clothes lines (Cat. E.15). Several of his Durham views, including this one, were engraved for Thomas Rose's publication of 1839, *Durham and Northumberland*.

Robert Pollard after James Edward Terry, *North Front View of Durham Cathedral* 1821, Cat. E.8.

George Winter after Robert William Billings, *Durham Cathedral, The Western Towers from the Windows of the Monks' Library* (1844), Cat. E.18.

While some artists sought to make the Cathedral picturesque or grandly ethereal in nature, others sought to show the more everyday, 'domestic' aspects of life in and around it (while continuing to omit representations of actual religious devotion). William Brown's two prints of 1809 taken from Framwellgate and Claypath give some prominence to the town in which the Cathedral sits, and include the first factory chimney (Cats. E.6 and E.7). A large-scale print by Robert Pollard after a drawing by James Terry of 1821 shows the north side of the Cathedral with families taking a stroll, a boy bowling his hoop and a flock of birds flying around the towers (Cat. E.8). Even Thomas Allom could also introduce an everyday conversation into his view of the Galilee Chapel (Cat. E.12).

Robert William Billings (already mentioned as an architectural draughtsman, p.25) most

G. Hawkins after W. R. Robinson, *Durham Cathedral and Castle from the North Road* (1846), Cat. E.21.

Rock & Co., *Durham from the Railway Station* and *Durham from the Battery* (1863), Cat. E.23.

successfully combined the mundane with the grand. He shows an artist (himself?) sketching the Cathedral from Mountjoy Hill (Cat. E.17.) and depicts an atmospheric view of the western towers seen through another part of the building, the delicate tracery of a window of the Monks' Library (Cat. E.18). He was fond of choosing unusual angles, as his head-on picture from opposite the Galilee Chapel demonstrates (Cat. E.19).

During the nineteenth century, the Cathedral was increasingly pictured as part of the City. Frederick Nash portrayed a smoky town climbing up to a stately crown of Castle and Cathedral (Cat E.22, a print taken from his own painting which is now in the National Gallery of Ireland). Hawkins' two lithographs of the 1840s, taken from pictures by Carmichael and Robinson, show busy scenes of smoking chimneys and a contemporary urban community, complete with gas works but, as yet, without the railway viaduct (Cats. E.20 and E.21).

The railway brought new tourists and new views. The vignettes published by Rock and Company in 1863 are entitled *Durham from the Railway Station* and *Durham from the Battery* (Cat. E.23) - both were viewpoints constructed within the previous ten years. The Cathedral beckons these viewers to a resort with crinolined ladies attended by railway porters; the modern age of the tourist has arrived.

Testing the Tourist

How much do we remember of the scene? How accurate are our memories? In 1980, Dr. Douglas Pocock, Reader in Geography at the University of Durham, undertook a research project asking people to anticipate, then compare, their photographic record of Durham Cathedral with the experience 'alive' in memory.

The research involved 'capturing' visitors after they had taken a photograph on the spot near to 'Scott's plaque' at the western end of Prebends' Bridge, between mid-morning and mid-afternoon on certain days in July and August 1980. All respondents were on holiday. Forty-nine out of a hundred photographers returned questionnaires designed to test and compare photographic record with memory recall. Their responses demonstrated that memory retains selectively, by forgetting what we do not need (or perhaps want) to remember; and by re-ordering, so that greater coherence may be created than was actually present on location.

The first of two sealed envelopes taken and opened away from Durham requested respondents to anticipate their photograph by sketching, within a supplied frame, the outline of the main features which they expected their photograph would show. Three prospects emerged:

    1. About half produced the expected, fuller view incorporating Cathedral, river and part of the distant medieval Framwellgate Bridge (illustration A).

    2. A further quarter drew a more restricted version by omitting the bridge and producing a cathedral-focussed sketch (illustration B).

    3. The remaining quarter drew a bridge-focussed sketch with the river between symmetrical banks, with a narrowing perspective on a centrally positioned Framwellgate Bridge (illustration C).

In one-fifth of the drawings, the Cathedral was more prominent than in reality (illustration D). A quarter of the sketches misjudged the number of cathedral towers - the majority depicting just two - although five opted for a single one.

Participants were asked for their comments. Generally, the evidence of the photograph was considered deficient - the real experience had been three-dimensional, offering a 'wider view' with 'no vertical or

horizontal limits to the vision'. The photograph in contrast was 'totally unable to convey the life of the scene'.

Most respondents felt that the experience and memory were superior to the photograph. A number of the fullest articulations came from overseas visitors - one from New Zealand:

'I am not disappointed in my photo, it came out well, but the memory of standing on the bridge is much fuller. The photo

shows none of the Prebends' Bridge, which the memory of the experience includes. The motion of people and boats and water, and the warmth of the sun are all part of the memory not included in the picture. The memory moves and lives, but the photo is stopped at an instant.'

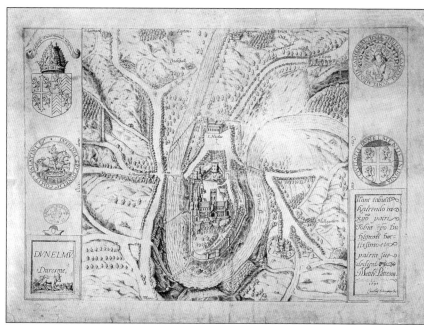

Christof Schwytzer, *Plan of the City of Durham* (1595), Cat. E.25.

Maps

Christof Schwytzer's map of 1595 dedicated to Matthew Patteson (now in a rather fragile state in the British Library) is the earliest map of Durham still in existence and shows an enclosed Cathedral City with hamlets outside (Cat.E.25). Everything is drawn '3-D', seen from a distance above.

In the first edition of John Speed's great Atlas, published 1610-11, Speed produced inset vignettes to accompany maps of over seventy towns, including Durham (Cat. E.26). The engravings were of a particularly high quality - Speed sent his manuscript maps over to Amsterdam and the plates were engraved there and returned to London for printing. His 'bird's-eye' view of Durham is well known from a wood-engraving print taken from it and inserted into Surtees' *History of the County Palatine of Durham* (Vol. IV), of 1840.

Forster and Mynde's map of 1754 (Cat. E.27) is full of detailed information. Much of it is drawn in plan form, but the Cathedral (and, to some extent, the Castle) is treated as a '3-D' composition. This element has been lost in Roper and Cole's version of 1804 where the Cathedral is now a flat plan. The 'artistic' element is achieved by placing a vignette of the Cathedral and Prebends' Bridge, engraved after Edward Dayes (see p. 15), in the top left-hand corner. An early form of calendar called *A Perpetual Table* shows a print of the mid-eighteenth century, with the times of sunrise and sunset for each day of the year (Cat. E. 29).

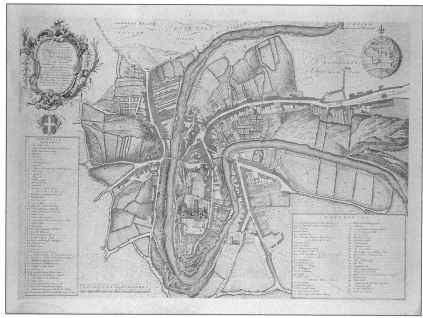

James Mynde after Thomas Forster, *Plan of the City of Durham* (1754), Cat. E.27.

HISTORIC AND MODERN

Watercolour was the medium for the great romantic visions and for architectural draughts-manship in the eighteenth century; it became increasingly used for smaller domestic scenes in the second half of the nineteenth century.

We are shown clerics crossing the College from their houses to the Cathedral (James Duffield Harding, Cat. F.1), a contrast to a watercolour by Billings of a similar scene which emphasises the architecture (Cat. F.4). Edmund Hastings, who could produce grand views in oil (Cat. C.8, see page 24) chose in some

of his watercolour sketches to show punters on the river and people relaxing on a walk (Cats. F.2, F.3). Harry Hine's smoky view of the City in 1881 is increasingly typical - the Cathedral seen as part of a landscape and a community (Cat.F.6). This 'composite' view of City and Cathedral is repeated by William Roxby Beverley in his *Durham Cathedral from the Prebends' Bridge* (Cat. F.5).

Fred Morgan was a local Durham man, running a business as a photographer and picture framer in Durham, in the 1890s. He produced a large

Edmund Hastings, *Durham* (1845), Cat. F.3.

number of sketches of the City (Cat. F.37) and published a collection entitled *Pen and Ink Sketches of Durham*.

The scale of many watercolours of this period is small and a certain 'tweeness' tends to creep into much of late Victorian painting. However, the smallest portrait ever made of Durham Cathedral is a simple composition in sepia by Sunderland-born artist Clarkson Stanfield. It shows the view from beneath Framwellgate Bridge (similar to that of Edward Dayes, illustrated p.15), on a miniature scale of 2.7 by 5.2 cms (about 1" by 2"), made for the Royal Dolls House at Windsor.

Artists painting in oils on a grander scale made great efforts to find original viewpoints. Typical of this consciously 'different' type of composition is W.R. Robinson's *Cathedral from Crossgate Peth* of 1844 (Cat. F.7, illustration page 36) which shows Pimlico in front of the Cathedral, viewed from

Edmund Hastings, *Durham Cathedral* (1841), Cat. F.2.

a high vantage point from the south-east. Robinson (1810-75) was a north-east artist who worked in Durham during the 1840s. Another view by him was engraved by Hawkins (Cat. E.21, p.32).

Clement Burlison (1803-1899) painted a very different *Durham* (Cat. F.8); here, the monument-ality of the Cathedral and Castle has to compete with the new railway viaduct constructed in 1857. In the foreground is Flass Vale (see George Fennel Robson's pre-viaduct view from the same spot, Cat. C.2). Burlison was a prolific painter of large-scale scenes, usually around Durham or in Italy; he came from County Durham and spent most of his life in the City after studying in London and travelling extensively in Europe. After his death, a room in Durham Town Hall became known as the Burlison Art Gallery, now the Members' Room. It houses selected paintings from the Burlison Bequest to the Corporation including the views by Robinson and Finn represented here. He is buried in St. Cuthbert's Churchyard.

In 1901 Herbert Finn was painting a very different *View of Framwellgate and the Cathedral* (Cat. F.9). It is smoky Durham, the Cathedral peering through a haze of coalsmoke from the multitude of roofs beneath. This is a painting on

W. R. Robinson, *View of the Cathedral from Crossgate Peth* (1844), Cat. F.7.

Clement Burlison, *Durham* (after 1857), Cat. F.8.

two planes - the mundane and the grand, in a consciously modern style. It was one of two Durham views he showed at St. James' Hall in 1902; the catalogue refers to 'a view of Durham over a screen of housetops, with a cloud of smoke and mist ... a well-balanced composition with fine contrasts of colour'. Finn's view is not unique: many late Victorian painters showed 'smoky' Durham, such as May Davidson of Sunderland in her two oils of the 1890s (in The College of St. Hild and St. Bede , Durham University), and Gerald Ackermann (1876 - 1960) whose watercolour (in Norfolk Museums Service) shows an almost smouldering City with the

Herbert John Finn, *View of Framwellgate and the Cathedral* (1901), Cat. F.9.

Cathedral silhouetted above it.

Other large-scale paintings of this period abound. An enormous oil painting by William McGregor entitled _Durham - Evening_ of 1903 hangs in Glasgow City Hall; George Reid's large oil painting of Durham in 1899 is held in Aberdeen Art Gallery. Other major watercolour views include several by William Callow (1812-1908) - now in Birmingham City collection and the National Gallery of Ireland; by Albert Goodwin, (1845-1932), an example of whose work is held by the Laing Art Gallery, Newcastle; and by Henry Charles Brewer (b.1866) whose large-scale watercolours seem to be rivalling oil paintings in their scale.

Richard A.Ray, _Durham City_ (1949), Cat. F.10.

In the period 1900-1950 most artists show a certain similarity of approach, portraying the Cathedral as part of the City, stressing its architectural and social interdependence with the Castle, the Peninsula and the crowded houses of Framwellgate, demolished in the 1930s. But they diverge in emphasising either the tranquil harmony of the location or its congested busyness.

Richard Ray's _Durham City_ (Cat. F.10) of 1949 shows a majestic medieval scene besieged by modern encroachments - two-way traffic ran across Framwellgate Bridge until the mid 1970s. Ray's style is careful and illustrative, and his rendering of the Cathedral and Castle above

Harold H. Holden, _Durham_ (1927), Cat. F.11.

would be rather dull without the human activity over the river. Similar compositions were produced by Kenneth Steel in his _Durham No. 1_ (Cat. F.12) which has a more schematic style, and Byron Dawson's _Durham Cathedral_ which shows a City crowded with buildings but empty of people (Cat. F.15).

By contrast, the limpid watercolours of Harold Holden and Leonard Squirrel show a silhouetted and theatrical scene, the Cathedral brooding majestically over the City. Harold Holden (1885-1977) produced at least two versions of his _Durham_ of 1927 (Cat.F.11). The one shown here is from Cheltenham Art Gallery; a more simplified version, in which the shapes of the buildings have become abstract blocks of colour washes, is held in Birmingham Art Gallery.

Leonard Squirrel's _Grey Day in Durham_ of 1939 (Cat.F.14) is actually rather more colourful than Holden's. It is one of several Durham watercolours and etchings made by this East Anglian watercolourist. He was influenced in his style by the flat watercolour wash of Cotman (see page 18) as were other artists of this period such as Francis Brodribb, whose _Distant View of Durham_ of 1933, similar in style to Leonard Squirrel's work, is held by Reading Museums and Art Gallery.

Illustration became a preoccupation of printmakers during the middle of this century. Graham Culverd's

Graham Culverd, *Durham*, Cat. F.16.

Peter Yates, *Durham Cathedral* (1976), Cat. F. 21.

Dennis Creffield, *The South West Towers from the Monks' Garden, The Galilee in the Foreground, Sunset* (1987), Cat. F. 22.

careful *Durham Cathedral* (Cat. F.16) is an example of the skill in detailing so typical of British etching of this period - and of the literalness which so often accompanied it! The prints of Henry Rushbury and Walter Lishman demonstrate a freer handling and a more determined effort to secure original vantage points. Lishman's *Durham Cathedral, from Court Lane* (Cat. F.18) looks up to the West end past houses and through trees; his *Durham* of 1971 is seen from the new Leazes Road built in 1967 (Cat. F.19).

The illustrative style was superseded by abstracted images such as Kenneth Rowntree's constructed image of wood and clay on a base of hessian and wood, entitled *West Front, Durham*, with its references to St. Carileph (Cat. F.20). By contrast, Peter Yates's view of *Durham Cathedral* from his study in the University is a schematic version which omits the religious aspect altogether, reducing the Cathedral to a two tone picture-within-a-picture, basically domestic in theme (Cat.F.21).

In the 1980s, serious artistic studies of the spirituality and monumentality of the Cathedral began to appear. Some artists were based within the Cathedral buildings themselves (see section G), some were visitors. Dennis Creffield was a visiting artist, but with a difference. In 1987, the South Bank commissioned him to draw all twenty-six medieval cathedrals of England. From February to November 1987, he travelled more than a thousand miles in a motor caravan, drawing in all weathers. The commission fulfilled a forty-year ambition and he wrote at the outset of his journey, 'No artist has ever

before drawn all the English medieval cathedrals - not even Turner. I've dreamt of doing so since I was 17...'. The resulting exhibition opened in 1988 and toured the country for two years, taking in many of the Cathedral cities (it was shown at Durham Art Gallery in November 1988). Creffield produced a large group of Durham drawings, including *The South West Towers from the Monks' Garden, The Galilee in the Foreground, Sunset* (Cat. F.22). They are large, monumental impressions of space, weight and looming power.

Birtley Aris' views from 1987 are monumental in a different way, being large-scale watercolours of the interior which explore colour and structure. They are taken from points with exciting perspectives, looking up or down at an angle, through arches and peering around pillars. The artist, a local north east resident, wished 'to represent the building with some accuracy...' but also 'to communicate the visual excitement of its massive Norman interior.' Unlike Creffield's summer visit, Aris chose to work in the autumn and winter to obtain rich shadows with a limited light source. Virtually all the work was done on the spot. The elongated shape of the pictures emphasises perspectives and light. *Bishop Cosin's Font Cover* (Cat.F.24) is lit up dramatically by the red of the stained glass window behind it.

Eleanor Bowen's interiors encompass both watercolours and charcoal drawings. Her *Triforium Pulley* of 1986 (Cat. F.25) conveys the massive solidity of the stone and the dimly lit passageways between it, and the weighty machinery needed to deal with repairs and movement in times gone by.

Valerie Thornton, *The Dun Cow* (1982), Cat. F.27.

Recent printmakers have approached the Cathedral in a wide variety of ways. Valerie Thornton specialised in rendering the texture of weathered walls and surfaces in ancient buildings, through the medium of etching. Her *Durham Cathedral, Interior* of 1982 (Cat. F.26) has few shadows but makes patterns of light on the stonework. The more playful *Dun Cow* (Cat. F.27) has the same grainy, textured surface.

Hilary Paynter's wood engraving of 1980 entitled *Durham* (Cat. F.29, illustrated on page 8) echoes seventeenth-century prints in its birds-eye view and its detailing - but she uses a very modern sense of design and perspective.

Birtley Aris, *Bishop Cosin's Font Cover in the west end of the nave* (1991), F.24.

David Gentleman, *Northern Solid Geometry* (1982), Cat. F.38.

Alyson McNeill's tiny woodcut of the Cathedral and Castle (Cat F.28, illustrated on title page) was commissioned by Durham University as a 'logo' for its Alumni Magazine in 1991.

Freddie Theys is a very different type of artist, a Belgian living and working near Antwerp, who was commissioned by Shotton's, the Durham printseller, to execute a series of etchings of Durham City in his characteristic linear style (Cat. F.30).

Few of the twentieth-century artists featured in this exhibition have created their work specifically for book reproduction. But David Gentleman painted a pillar of Durham Cathedral for his own *David Gentleman's Britain*, published in 1982; he makes a visual pun of the pillar, taking a 'half-slice' and juxtaposing it with a Ferrybridge powerstation cooling tower - two views in one with the title of *Northern Solid Geometry* (Cat.F.38). His characteristically ebullient prose describes the pillar motifs, 'diamonds, zig-zags, barber-pole spirals,' curving round with a 'child-like simplicity, directness and self-confidence'.

Durham Cathedral is a much-photographed building. Royston Thomas is a local professional photographer whose black-and-white compositions are familiar in the City (Cat. F.31). Angelo Hornak is a London-based professional specialising in illustrative work; he was commissioned to make a series of colour prints to illustrate Deborah Shipley's book, *Durham Cathedral* (Cats. F.33, F.34). John Erskine is a local amateur photographer whose *Romanesque Reflection* won a prize in Durham Photographic Society's centenary exhibition at the Art Gallery in 1992 (Cat. F.32).

Stained glass is found in profusion as part of the Cathedral building itself. Simon Whistler, the eminent glass engraver, has produced a *Durham Cathedral Goblet* specifically for this exhibition (Cat. F.36).

Valerie Thornton, *Durham Cathedral, Interior* (1982), Cat. F.26.

THE CATHEDRAL ARTISTS-IN-RESIDENCE

In 1970, the Cathedral's Chaplaincy to the Arts and Recreation converted a former rectory in Teesside into a centre for artists of all disciplines to meet and work together. One experiment within this centre was the provision for an Artist-in-Residence, financially supported and monitored by Northern Arts for possible development elsewhere. Some ten years later and with the combined support of a variety of sponsors, the Chaplaincy was able to develop the Residency from a base within the precincts of Durham Cathedral itself.

The two-fold purpose of the Residency is the same as it was when the first artist was appointed in 1983. It is to provide time and space for an artist, free of all other pressures, to respond to the Cathedral as a powerful creative statement in stone, a place of daily worship, and the centre of a working community of stone masons, joiners, gardeners and office workers, as well as vergers, musicians and clergy; and to provide the opportunity for public access to an artist at work.

Not all the works shown here were produced during the artists' Residencies, nor do all depict the Cathedral, for several used their stay as a stimulus to their own themes and preoccupations, as well as a continuing interest in the building itself. For several, the Residency presented a significant artistic challenge, best expressed by Jo Burns, who wrote in her application for the Residency:

> 'The image of Durham, the Cathedral, the river, the famous silhouette against the sky - all are familiar. The problem would be one of seeing these aspects anew, to find a way to the subject which would transcend the cliché of the picturesque and give to the subject the resonance and dignity it deserves.'

Jo Burns, *Sketch: Durham Cathedral looking South East* (1991), Cat. G.5.

Virginia Bodman, *Red Column* (1987), Cat. G.3.

Most of the artists worked on a very large scale. Due to restrictions of space, only small works can be shown in this exhibition. (In 1996, the north-east's year of the Visual Arts, a major exhibition at Durham Art Gallery will feature more fully all the Artists-in-Residence).

Virginia Bodman was the first Resident. She worked in a variety of media and styles - large oils exploring the motifs of the Cathedral, drawings, line prints and oils; *The Red Column* is a small, glowing oil painting from 1988 (Cat. G.3). Flick Allen's large scale pictures are imaginary episodes set in the Cathedral, mingling the architectural elements with religious imagery (*Three Figures in Durham Cathedral*, Cat. G.2). Anita Taylor and Gerald Davies both concentrated on the human figure, also taking mystical themes in *Seeking Sanctuary* (Cat. G.4) and *Carving an Icon* (Cat. G.1). Matthew Carey produced figurative and non-figurative work in charcoal drawings; his *Candelabra* is a portrait of one small element of the Cathedral, charged with a sense of symbolism (Cat. G.6). Tara Sabharwal's small mysterious drawings, such as *Magic* (G.7) explore a mystical world in dreamlike scenes. Jo Burns was fascinated by the setting of the Cathedral, explored in a series of large works - a group of tiny oil sketches is featured in this exhibition (Cat. G.5). The current Artist-in-Residence, Richard Cole, produces both atmospheric etchings (Cat. G.8) and sculptures (Cat. G.9).

Two other Artists-in-Residence were sculptors, both very different in their approach. Colin Wilbourn works in wood: his rectangular *Last Supper Table* (Cat. G.11) - one of three sculptures produced from the Residency - opens up to show an inlaid patterned cross. The table is made from oak beams removed from the Cathedral belfry during restoration in the 1980s. Deborah Gardner's *Guardian Angel* (Cat. G.10) is a simple figure, far removed from the conventional Victorian-Gothic image of winged dignity and splendour.

The Artists-in-Residence

Virginia Bodman	1984-1985
Flick Allen	1985-1986
Matthew Carey	1986-1987
Colin Wilbourn	1987-1988
Anita Taylor	1988-1989
Gerald Davies	1989-1990
Tara Sabharwal	1990-1991
Jo Burns	1991-1992
Deborah Gardner	1992-1993
Richard Cole	1993-1994

Matthew Carey, *Candelabra* (1986), Cat. G.6.

H

SYMBOLS AND SIGNS

Railway Posters

From their formation in 1923, the four main railway companies used spectacular posters to advertise their routes. Large and colourful, they were generally produced in a limited range of bright colours for ease of colour lithography printing.

Fred Taylor (1875-1963) was one of the leading exponents of posters for the London and North Eastern Railway (LNER). His *Durham: It's Quicker by Rail* (Cat. H.3) shows a wooded, country image, homely and almost cosy with only the rooftops of houses peeping above the trees. Here, the Cathedral *is* Durham. By contrast in his interior view, *Durham* (Cat. H.4), all is grandeur and magnificence; again, the Cathedral stands for the City. Taylor's posters were made from full-scale paintings. He exhibited at the Royal Academy and other art galleries as well as becoming LNER's most prolific artist.

Frank Brangwyn was an artist whose work was occasionally translated into poster form (see illustration above). Other LNER poster designs included a *Durham* with a frieze of figures based on medieval manuscripts, by Doris Zinkeisen, published in 1932.

Frank Brangwyn, *Durham: It's Quicker by Rail*, (not in exhibition)

Fred Taylor, *Durham: Cathedral Interior* (c. 1930), Cat. H. 4.

A. F. Kersting's poster of 1953, *Durham: See Britain by Train*, continues to feature the Cathedral as the symbol for the region (Cat. H.5). The poster is based on a monochrome photograph, overprinted in the studio with colour washes. It emphasises the rural aspect of the area - there is no hint of a city at all.

Far left: Fred Taylor, *Durham: It's Quicker by Rail* (c.1930), Cat. H.3.
Left: A. F. Kersting *Durham* (1953), Cat. H.5.

Trade Union Banners

Trade Union banners are one of the best examples of popular art. In the 1830s, when few could read, the miners' banner was not just a colourful rallying point but an important means for miners and their families to pick out their lodge at the Gala or at the local rallies. But, as A.W. Moyes points out in his *Banner Book* of 1974, it is only recently that they have come to be regarded as a popular art form; the 1973 exhibition in Durham Art Gallery 'was perhaps the first indoor exhibition of Trades Union banners in the world' (Moyes, page 7). Over a dozen banners have used the Cathedral image, and since the average life of a banner tends to be about twenty years, some lodges have had five or six each - there may be many now unrecorded.

Banner of the County Durham Branch of the National Union of Agricultural Workers (1948), Cat. H.2.

Traditionally, banners were made of pure silk woven in London by the descendants of Huguenot silk weavers. The firm of George Tutill had most of the trade; in 1861, he took out a patent for coating silk with India rubber and linseed oil, making the image flexible and colourfast. The paintings were the work of highly specialised craftsmen - one painting faces, one mottoes, one landscapes and so on. As they were being painted, the banners were stretched onto a frame and tilted forward so that splashes would fall to the floor.

The two banners shown here, both held at Beamish, the North of England Open Air Museum, belong to the Brancepeth Miners' Lodge and the County Durham Branch of the National Union of Agricultural Workers (Cats. H.1, H.2).

The picture on the front of the *Brancepeth Banner* is entitled 'The Big Meeting' and shows the Durham Miners' Gala in the foreground alongside the River Wear. The Cathedral is the 'backdrop' or symbol for the County. On the reverse is an illustration of Burnhope Reservoir, an unusual type of subject. It is a tribute to miners' leader and local politician Peter Lee, who undertook the creation of the reservoir during his Chairmanship of the Durham County Water Board (both sides are illustrated side by side in Moyes ' book, page 138).

The *Agricultural Workers Banner* shows a much more rural view of Durham - a green countryside scene with a backdrop of the Cathedral and Castle in pale coloured stone. The design is taken from an engraving by Saddler after R.W. Billings (see p.26) published in 1841. It is probably a Tutill banner, and the pattern of the red and orange damask is similar to the Miners' Banner in reverse. On the back of the banner is an image of plough horses and plough, the symbol of the Union of Agricultural Workers.

Carriage Prints

Carriage prints - small reproductions of photographs or paintings placed above seats in railway compartments - are rare now in Britain (though still in use in underground trains). Artists had to work to an odd size of approximately 15cm x 41cm (6" x 16") which encouraged long panoramic views. Leading artists were employed on these projects despite the restrictions of format; the fine art aspect was emphasised by the inscription 'From a Watercolour by...' beneath the image. In depicting Durham, licence was taken with perspectives, as comparisons with photographs from the same viewpoints show.

Edwin Byatt, *Durham Cathedral*, Cat. H.6.

Edwin Byatt's *Durham Cathedral* takes a conventional leafy view from above Prebends' Bridge, curiously omitting the Castle (Cat. H.6). By contrast the townscapes of John Moody and Sidney Causer show the city buildings climbing up to the pinnacle of the Cathedral and Castle (Cats. H.7 and H.8). Moody's unusual north view is taken from outside the present Northern Electric building and shows the start of the Ice Rink (in 1938/9); the rink was completed in 1942 and now blocks part of the view. Moody worked as an etcher and the detailed, linear quality of the style reflects this approach. His use of a restricted colour range is interesting - the contrast between the blue-grey of the Cathedral and the brown of the Castle creates two distinct structures although the towers of the Cathedral rise behind the Castle walls.

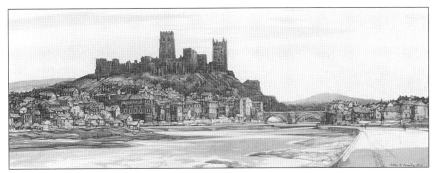

John C. Moody, *Durham* (1938-9), Cat. H.7.

Sidney Causer, *Durham*, Cat. H.8.

Sidney Causer takes a north-north-east view from Old Elvet tow path with Elvet Bridge in the foreground. It is a more domestic town portrait with the main Cathedral tower and Castle peering above the houses.

Postcards

There are so many postcards to chose from that only a small selection of the older ones are shown here, all drawn from the extensive collection of David Williams (Cat. H.9). There are monochrome and hand-coloured photographs, oil paintings and

Postcard: H. B. Wimbush, *Durham* (1914-18), Cat. H.9. (iv)

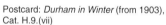

Postcard: *Durham in Winter* (from 1903), Cat. H.9.(vii)

drawings specially made for photographic reproduction, a comic 'pop-up' pun of 1913 and a violently coloured orange, black and silver design with the view from the railway station which looks surprisingly modern for the early 1900s. Durham Cathedral under snow has always been a favourite theme and one shows people on the frozen river, probably in the severe winter of 1899.

The photographic images of the 1960s and 1970s are rather prosaic, but a new 'art' consciousness appears in the late 1980s using silhouetted outlines, carefully controlled colour schemes and a limited tonal range (Cat. H.10).

Postcard: Robert Weil, *Durham Between Heaven and Hell* (current), Cat. H.10.

Images of Durham Cathedral abound as decorative symbols and commercial logos. One appeared on a 5d. postage stamp in 1969 (Cat. H.11), in a set of six 'Cathedral' images designed by Peter Gauld and issued on 28th May 1969.

'Cathedral Series' Postage Stamp (1969), Cat. H.11.

Postal Franking, Pitney Bowes (1990), Cat. H.12.

A postal franking from Pitney Bowes was commissioned by the Dean and Chapter in 1990.

The Cathedral was once featured on a five-pound Durham banknote, along with Prebends' Bridge and a mythical maiden sitting on a stone inscribed 'Darlington'. The example featured here was issued by Jonathan Backhouse and Company, Sunderland, around 1830 (Cat. H.13).

The Cathedral image was used on a wide variety of commercial items, often as one of a series of Cathedrals or other historic buildings. Around 1800, Spode produced a Landscape Dessert Service which included a Durham Cathedral. Around 1825-30, Minton's produced a bone china Potpourri Bowl with the Cathedral

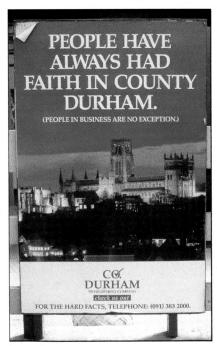

Wedgwood 'Cathedral Series' dessert plate (1930), Cat. H.14.

depicted on its side (an example, too fragile to travel, is now held in the National Museum of Wales). In 1930, a plate was produced as one of Wedgwood's 'Cathedral Series' of Catherine Shape LNER Souvenir Dessert Plates (Cat. H.14). It is hardly original in design - a view from Prebends' Bridge with the Fulling Mill and boathouse in the foreground. The series was made in the same shape and earthenware material as the famous service made for Empress Catherine II of Russia in 1774, with the borders in the same style but with the rose and thistle of the LNER Coat of Arms. Others in the series were Ely, Lincoln, Norwich, Peterborough and York, all places accessible to travellers on LNER railways.

C.T. Maling and Sons, the North East potters, produced a 'Cathedrals' Tea Caddy for Ringtons Ltd, Tea and Coffee Merchants of Newcastle in 1929 (Cat.H.15). They were originally produced for the North-East Coast Industries Exhibition. A miniature version was made by Wade Potteries, Stoke on Trent, in 1989 (Cat. H.16). These earthenware caddies are hexagonally shaped with blue and white transfer prints; there is also a metal version. Other designs included local bridges and castles.

Mauchline Ware is a type of wooden giftware, made in Mauchline, Scotland, from the 1850s to the 1930s. One example was a glassholder with a view of Durham from the Railway Station (Cat. H.17). These wooden items were made of pale, close-grained wood (usually sycamore) with transfer-printed pen

County Durham Development Company Poster (1990) at Durham Station (photo Cat. H.19(g).)

drawings fixed on with oil copal varnish.

Many other non-souvenir items also bear the image of the Cathedral. The *Northumberland Quilt* (Cat. H.19) is a symbol of the region of Northumbria and bears an image of the Cathedral in its corner. Completed in 1987 by a group of Northumbrian craftswomen and artists, it is dedicated to St. Cuthbert and to the glories of Historic Northumbria; it honours the Queen Mother, whose signature graces the quilt.

One craftswoman, Mrs. Fellowes, used a Cathedral motif, the *Sanctuary Ring*, as the subject of a sculpture in corn. Mr. Fred Draper produced a sculpture of Durham Cathedral about six feet long, entirely in matchsticks; he presented it to the Cathedral in 1986 and it is currently on public view in the Monks' Dormitory. Marilyn Hopkins, working in Durham Art Gallery with members of the public in 1992, made a traditional hooky rug using the *Sanctuary Ring* motif. Kit embroideries of *Durham Cathedral* were produced by the Anchor Company in the 1950s in very large numbers: the various scenes produced of British towns and buildings were worked in brown thread on a cream base (Cat. H.18).

Photographers have used the Cathedral as a motif for specific purposes. Royston Thomas generally takes serious portraits of the Cathedral and City (Cat. F.31) but he makes a visual pun with a photograph of a fruitcake overlaying one of the East Window, entitled *Feast Window*. County Durham Development Company, in their recent promotional poster, used a straightforward floodlit night scene of the Cathedral but added the motto, 'People have always had faith in County Durham (People in business are no exception)' - it has greeted visitors at stations and airports and has been featured in magazines worldwide (Cat. H. 19).

In addition, there are numerous calendars, sketchbooks, pub signs and other visual representations. For this exhibition, a schools competition was held to design a flag to fly outside the gallery. The winner was Lindsey McCormick, aged 7, of Ushaw Moor Junior School (Cat. F.35).

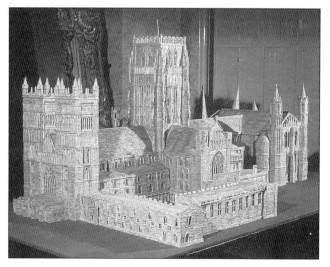

Fred Draper, *Matchstick Model of Cathedral*, (1986) (photo Cat. H.19(c).)

LOOKING TO THE PAST

Visions of the past change from one later age to another. A hundred years ago, the 'Walter Scott' image of romanticism coloured the imagination. A good example of this is the work of Newcastle artist Ralph Hedley, entitled *Seeking Sanctuary* (Cats. I.l, I.2, I.3), a melodramatic image of a handsome young criminal who is clearly expected to gain our sympathy rather than censure for any possible wrong-doing. Ralph Hedley (1848 - 1913) worked entirely in a narrative style, usually depicting contemporary life in the north east. As noted by John Millard (in his book accompanying the exhibition *Ralph Hedley: Tyneside Painter*, Laing Art Gallery, Newcastle, 1990), *Seeking Sanctuary* was a new departure for Hedley in that it represented the historic past. The inspiration came from the *Monthly Chronicle of North-Country Folklore and Legend* of 1889 and the picture enjoyed great success at both the Bewick Club in Newcastle and the Royal Academy in London. The original (Cat. I.l) is now in

Ralph Hedley, Photogravure of *Seeking Sanctuary*, Cat. I.3.

an Australian collection, though brought here for this exhibition; the oil sketch is in the Laing Art Gallery (Cat. I.2) and a photogravure was produced for sale (Cat. I.3).

Representation of the sanctuary custom may not be accurate but the picture does tell a *story* - a typical feature of Victorian historical representation. The twelfth-century Sanctuary Ring (kept in the Cathedral Treasury - the one now on the North Door is a replica) could be used by any criminal seeking asylum. Two watchmen stayed each night in a chamber above the door to admit criminals and tolled the bell to

Ronald Embleton, *Durham, South West Prospect* (1980s), Cat. I. 9.

let the City know that someone was seeking sanctuary. Even in 1890, the picture aroused both praise and derision - *Punch* retitled it 'Coming Home Late in the Olden Time. No latch key...'.

Bathed in strong moonlight, the fugitive still clutches his sword - though no criminal could claim sanctuary bearing his weapons.

Ronald Embleton has taken further the careful, accurate representation of Durham in the past, fleshing out prints of the eighteenth century in his *Durham, South West Prospect* (Cat. I.9) and of the nineteenth century in his *North Side from Framwellgate, circa 1840* (Cat. I.10).

Alan Sorrell (1904-1974) made his living out of 'reconstruction' paintings, mainly of archaeological sites. His work is used in books, displays and noticeboards at historical sites. The powerful drawing of the Cathedral Nave was made as a page for the book *Norman Britain* published for children in 1966 (Cat. I.4).

The largest picture of the Cathedral ever painted is the Tom Pattison's mural commissioned for Durham County Council in the 1960s, which measures around 1.98 x 7.02 metres (6' 6" x 23'). It is located in the Durham Room at County Hall, Durham and depicts *The Building of Durham Cathedral*. The preliminary bodycolour sketch for it is shown here (Cat.I.8). Pattison taught at the School of Art, King's College, Newcastle, and in Hexham, but also worked on a wide number of commissions. His vision is a very clean, idealised version, a story-book narrative in the colour scheme of children's books of his time.

Ronald Embleton, *Durham Cathedral, North Side from Framwellgate* (1980s), Cat. I. 10.

Selwyn Beattie is a local designer and school teacher. In the early 1980s he chaired the Cathedral's Craftsmen for Christ exhibition, designing exhibits and illustrations and producing a series of sketches for the Durham Cathedral Schools Pack. These large-scale, monochrome drawings were reproduced in pamphlets and fact sheets. They are practical explanations of how the Cathedral was made with no effort wasted on historical atmosphere (Cats. I.5, I.6). In fact, Beattie seems to have made a positive virtue of making his figures as timeless as

Thomas Pattison, '*The Building of Durham' Mural*, *County Hall, Durham,* (see Cat. I.8.)

possible. He takes a slightly more stylistic approach in his modestly titled *Durham Cathedral as it may have appeared in the Twelfth Century* (Cat. I.7) with its dramatic sky and low viewpoint.

left: Selwyn S. Beattie, *Construction of Durham Cathedral Pillars* (1983), Cat. I.6.

below: Selwyn S. Beattie, *Durham Cathedral as it may have appeared in the Twelfth Century* (1976), Cat. I.7.

However awe-inspiring the Cathedral itself, it is the total effect of the building and the setting combined which has been such an enduring inspiration to artists; as J.N. Brewer wrote in *The History and Antiquities of the Cathedral Church of Durham* in 1819,

> 'The cathedral-church of Durham is seated on a rocky eminence, which forms the highest part of the city. Owing to this singularity of situation, the building is viewed with an impressive sublimity of effect from many points of observation.'

Robert Raymond, *The Site of Durham
Cathedral*, 20.0 x 18.8 cms (not in exhibition)

LIST OF EXHIBITS

Note: all items are on paper unless stated otherwise. The sizes are given in centimetres, height before width. Where the image has a defined border, (such as a print) the size given is that of the border.

In some cases, it has not been possible to check size and medium before going to print.

Space permits only a brief Checklist of items and a full Catalogue Raisonné has not been attempted.

Abbreviations:

MSS	Additional Manuscripts collection of the British Museum
b.	born
c.	circa (approximate date)
cms	centimetres
d.	died
fl.	flourished/working period

A. EARLY IMAGES

A.1. **Daniel King**
The North Prospect of the Cathedral Church of Durham
1656
Etching
19.8 x 29.8 cms
Durham University Library
Illus. p.11

A.2. **Daniel King**
The East Prospect of the Cathedral Church of Durham
1656
Etching
25.0 x 17.2 cms
Durham University Library
Illus. p.11

A.3. **Daniel King**
South view of Durham Cathedral   1655
Etching
17.4 x 30.3 cms
Durham University Library

A.4. **Daniel King**
The West Prospect of the Cathedral Church of Durham
1656
Etching
26.2 x 17.2 cms
Durham University Library
Illus. p.10

A.5. **Anon**
The South-West Prospect of the City of Durham 1749
Etching
17.4 x 24.4 cms
Durham University Library

A.6. **Anonymous artist (after Buck)**
Perspective View of the Cathedral and City of Durham, in the County of Durham   (before 1771)
Etching
15.6 x 27.6 cms
Durham University Library
Illus. p.13

A.7. **James Mynde** after **Thomas Forster**
An East View of Durham from Pelloe-Wood-Hill 1754
Engraving
24.0 x 33.7 cms
Sunderland Museum and Art Gallery (Tyne and Wear Museums)

A.8. **John Clerk of Eldin**
Durham Cathedral   1774-5
Etching and drypoint
18.9 x 30.1 cms
Sunderland Museum and Art Gallery (Tyne and Wear Museums)

A.9. **Samuel Buck**
Durham Cathedral   (early 18th century)
Oil on canvas
74.5 x 108.5 cms
The Dean and Chapter of Durham
Illus. p.11

A.10. **(?) Samuel Buck**
Durham Cathedral and Castle, with Bishop's Barge
Oil on canvas
139.7 x 222.2 cms
Private British Collection
Illus. p.12

A.11. **Anonymous artist**
Panorama of Durham City and Environs   (c1700)
Grisaille painting in oil on canvas
152.4 x 242.6 cms
Private British Collection
Illus. p.12

A.12. **Samuel Hieronymous Grimm**
North View up the River Wear at Durham
Grey wash over pen and black ink
18.5 x 27.0 cms
Inscribed with title
British Library Add MSS 15538, f.129
Illus. p.14

A.13. **Samuel Hieronymous Grimm**
Distant View of Durham
Grey wash over pen and black ink
18.5 x 27.0 cms
British Library Add MSS 15538, f.130

A.14. **Samuel Hieronymous Grimm**
The New Dun Cow at Durham
Grey wash over pen and black ink
18.5 x 26.0 cms
Inscribed with title
British Library Add MSS 15538, f.135

A.15. **Samuel Hieronymous Grimm**
Thorntree and Dun Cow at Durham
Grey wash over pen and black ink
27.0 x 18.5 cms
Inscribed with title
British Library Add MSS 15538, f.137

A.16. **Samuel Hieronymous Grimm**
The Dean's Kitchen
Pen and black ink
25.0 x 24.0 cms
Inscribed with title
British Library Add MSS 15538, f.166

A.17. **Samuel Hieronymous Grimm**
Durham from the River   1779
Watercolour with pencil and ink
33.5 x 51.6 cms
Signed and dated
Laing Art Gallery (Tyne and Wear Museums)

A. 18. **Samuel Hieronymous Grimm**
Celebration of Communion
Grey wash over pen and ink
18.8 x 27.2 cms (sight size)
The Dean and Chapter of Durham

B. THE PICTURESQUE

B.1. **Edward Blore**
Durham Cathedral: West Front
Brown wash over pencil, with white heightening
32.0 x 21.0 cms
British Library Add MSS 42016, f.1
Illus. p.16

B.2. **Edward Blore**
Durham Cathedral: Choir, looking East
Grey wash over pencil, with white heightening
32.5 x 21.5 cms
British Library Add MSS 42016, f.3

B.3. **Edward Dayes**
*Durham Cathedral from beneath an Arch of Ralph
Flambard's Bridge: Moonlight*   1797
Watercolour over pencil
10.7 x 16.2 cms
Signed and dated
The Visitors of the Ashmolean Museum, Oxford
Illus. p.15

B.4. **William Daniell**
Durham Cathedral   1805
Watercolour
40.0 x 65.1cms
Signed and dated
The Board of Trustees of the
Victoria and Albert Museum
Illus. p.15

B.5. **John Pearson**
View of Durham Cathedral from the River
Watercolour
26.7 x 32.7 cms
The Board of Trustees of the
Victoria and Albert Museum

B.6. **Thomas Girtin**
Durham Cathedral   1796-99
Watercolour
46.9 x 41.2 cms
Trustees of the British Museum
Illus. p.16

B.7. **Joseph Mallord William Turner**
Durham Cathedral   (c1799)
Watercolour
30.4 x 40.6 cms
Signed
Royal Academy of Arts
Illus. p.17

B.8. **John Sell Cotman**
View of Durham from the North West
Watercolour over pencil
44.6 x 58.5 cms
Trustees of the British Museum
Illus. p. 19

B.9. **John Sell Cotman**
Durham Cathedral   1806
Watercolour over pencil
43.6 x 33.0 cms
Trustees of the British Museum
Illus. p.19

B.10. **John Glover**
Durham Cathedral
Oil on canvas
72.8 x 102.2 cms
The Dean and Chapter of Durham
Illus. p.19

B.11. **Felix Mendelssohn-Bartholdy**
Durham Cathedral   1829
29.5 x 24.5 cms
Photograph of original in the Staatsbibliothek
Preussischer Kulturbesitz, Mendelssohn-Archiv, Berlin
(Original, 26.0 x 21.0 cms, water- colour and body
colour)
Illus. p. 20

C.   THE GRAND VIEW

C.1.   George Fennel Robson
Durham
Watercolour
56.0 x 84.0 cms
Colonel. S.J. Furness

C.2.   George Fennel Robson
Durham Cathedral and Castle
Watercolour
20.1 x 36.9 cms
The Board of Trustees of the Victoria & Albert Museum

C.3.   George Fennel Robson
Durham Cathedral and Castle from across the River
32.3 x 49.0 cms
The Visitors of the Ashmolean Museum, Oxford
Illus. p.21

C.4.   George Fennel Robson
Durham Cathedral from Prebends' Bridge
Watercolour
47.2 x 77.5 cms
Bowes Museum, Durham County Council
Illus. front cover

C.5.   George Fennel Robson
Durham
20.7 x 38.5 cms
Watercolour and bodycolour
Laing Art Gallery (Tyne & Wear Museums)
Illus. p. 21

C.6.   John Dobbin
Durham   (1854)
Watercolour
76.2 x 132.1 cms
Borough of Darlington Art Collections
Illus. p.22

C.7.   John Wilson Carmichael
Durham   (?1841)
Oil on canvas
60.7 x 91.6 cms
Signed and dated
Laing Art Gallery (Tyne and Wear Museums)
Illus. p.23

C.8.   Edmund Hastings
Cathedral Choir, Assize Sunday 1835
Oil on canvas
146.5 x 111.6 cms
The Dean and Chapter of Durham
Illus. p.24

C.9.   John Wilson Carmichael
Durham Cathedral and Castle   1847
Oil on canvas
Signed and dated
88.3 x 126.3 cms
Private British Collection

D.   ARCHITECTS AND ANTIQUARIANS

D.1.   James Wyatt
Plans for Durham Cathedral 1795:
Elevation of the East End
25th September 1795
Pencil Drawing
Signed and dated
Bound in Book, 53.8 x 66.5 cms
The Dean and Chapter of Durham
Illus. p.27

D.2.   John Carter
Some account of the Cathedral Church of Durham;
Illustrative of the Plans, Elevations and Sections of That
Building: Plate IV, Elevation of the North Front   1801
Double page from Book, 60.5 x 95.1 cms
The Dean and Chapter of Durham
Illus. p.25

D. 3 .   R. Reeve after **John Buckler**
North West View of the Cathedral Church of Durham
(1809)
Engraving
43.3 x 60.9 cms
The Dean and Chapter of Durham
Illus. p.27

D. 4.   John Saddler after **Robert William Billings**
Durham Cathedral. Elevation of the West Front   1843
Engraving and etching
22.4 x 15.5 cms
Sunderland Museum and Art Gallery (Tyne and Wear
Museums)
Illus. p.26

D. 5.   John Henry Le Keux after **Robert William Billings**
Durham Cathedral. North View from Framwellgate
1842
Engraving and etching
20.9 x 14.5 cms
Sunderland Museum and Art Gallery (Tyne and Wear
Museums)

D.6.   John Le Keux after **Robert William Billings**
Durham Cathedral. East View, from Bow Lane   1842
Engraving and etching
20.9 x 15.8 cms
Sunderland Museum and Art Gallery (Tyne and Wear
Museums)

D.7.   John Saddler after **Robert William Billings**
Durham Cathedral. Chapel of the Nine Altars Groining:
South End
Engraving and etching
17.3 x 22.0 cms
Sunderland Museum and Art Gallery (Tyne and Wear
Museums)
Illus. p.26

D.8. **John Saddler** after **Robert William Billings**
Durham Cathedral. Triforium of the Nave - North Side
1842
Engraving and etching
16.0 x 21.0 cms
Sunderland Museum and Art Gallery (Tyne and Wear
Museums)
Illus. p.26

D.9. **Robert William Billings**
*Illustrations of the Architectural Antiquities of the County
of Durham: ecclesiastical, castellated, and domestic*
(1846)
published in Durham by George Andrews and Robert
William Billings, and in London by T. & W. Boone
Book, 28.8 x 22.2 cms
The Dean and Chapter of Durham

D.10. **Giles Gilbert Scott**
Design for a Spire, Durham Cathedral   1859-60
Ink sketch
46.0 x 58.0 cms
The Dean and Chapter of Durham
Illus. p.28

D.11. **Anonymous artist**
The Cathedral in 1133   1862
Engraving on paper
8.7 x 18.0 cms
Print from *The Ecclesiologist*, vol.XX
'Karileph's Church'
The Dean and Chapter of Durham

D.12. **Francis Bedford**
Bishop Hatfield's Tomb   1893
Page from *The Builder*, 3 June 1893, from a pencil
drawing
25.3 x 18.5 cms (within border)
Durham University Library

D.13. **Mark Thompson**
*The Bishop's Throne in Durham Cathedral , 'shewing
the ancient colouring and gilding before it was defaced
in the year 1811'*   1836
Watercolour
32.5 x 21.0 cms
Signed and dated
The Dean and Chapter of Durham
Illus. p.28

D.14. **Sir J. Ninian Comper**
*Durham Cathedral, Design for Tester and Standard
Candlesticks for the Shrine of St. Cuthbert*   1947
Pencil drawing
43.3 x 25.9 cms (sight size)
The Dean and Chapter of Durham

D.15. **Sir Reginald T. Blomfield**
*Sketchbook 5: Sanctuary Knocker and South West
View*
Sketch
Sketchbook, 24.4 x 26.5 cms
Royal Institute of British Architects

D.16. **Ian Curry**
*Sense and Sensitivity: Durham Cathedral and its
Architects*   1985
Booklet published by the Dean and Chapter of Durham
21.0 x 14.7 cms

D.17. **Ian Curry**
*Aspects of the Anglo-Norman Design of Durham
Cathedral*   1986
Booklet published from the Society of Antiquaries of
Newcastle upon Tyne's journal *Archaeologia Aeliana*
24.9 x 18.9 cms
Illus. p.28

E. PRINTMAKERS AND TRAVELLERS

E.1. **Sparrow** after **Moses Griffiths**
The Cathedral Church and Bridge of Durham   1776
Engraving
14.6 x 20.2 cms
Durham University Library
Illus. p. 29

E.2. **(? Thomas) Thornton**
*View of the Cathedral Church of Durham in the County
of Durham*   1786
Engraving
8.1 x 14.7 cms
Durham University Library
Illus. p.29

E.3. **Francis Chesham** and **Frederick Duncannon** after
Paul Sandby
Durham   1780
Engraving
13.3 x 18.6 cms
The Dean and Chapter of Durham

E.4. **James Storer** after **Edward Dayes**
Durham   1796
Engraving
11.0 x 16.7 cms
Durham University Library
Illus. p.29

E.5. **William Angus** after **Edward Dayes**
Durham   1801
Engraving
9.4 x 15.2 cms
Durham University Library
Illus. p.29

E.6.	**William Brown**
Durham, From the Lower End of Framwell Gate 1809
Etching with aquatint
22.7 x 30.4 cms
Durham University Library

E.7.	**William Brown**
Durham, From the Upper Part of ClayPath	1809
Etching with aquatint
22.4 x 34.7 cms
The Dean and Chapter of Durham
Illus. p. 31

E.8.	**Robert Pollard** after **James Edward Terry**
North Front View of Durham Cathedral	1821
Engraving, aquatint and etching
36.3 x 58.0 cms
Sunderland Museum and Art Gallery (Tyne and Wear Museums)
Illus. p. 31

E.9.	**John Le Keux** after **George Fennel Robson**
North East View of the City of Durham	1828
Engraving
11.0 x 19.3 cms
Durham University Library
Illus. p.30

E.10.	**Edward Finden** after **George Fennel Robson**
Durham	1832
Engraving
8.2 x 11.8 cms
Durham University Library

E.11.	**W. Winkles and W. Taylor** after **George Fennel Robson**
North West View of the City of Durham	1828
Engraving, etching and watercolour
14.8 x 24.7 cms
Sunderland Museum and Art Gallery (Tyne and Wear Museums)

E.12.	**James Redaway** after **Thomas Allom**
The Galilee, West End of Durham Cathedral
Engraving
10.0 x 15.3 cms
Durham University Library
Illus. p.30

E.13.	**William Le Petit** after **Thomas Allom**
Durham from the North East	1834
Engraving
9.8 x 15.5 cms
Durham University Library

E.14.	**E. Young** after **Thomas Allom**
Interior of Durham Cathedral from the Nine Altars 1835
Engraving
15.1 x 10.1 cms
Durham University Library
Illus. p.30

E.15.	**Ebenezer Challis** after **Thomas Allom**
Durham	1832
Engraving
9.8 x 15.4 cms
Durham University Library

E.16.	**William Miller** after **Joseph Mallord William Turner**
Durham Cathedral	1836
Engraving with etching
15.7 x 23.5 cms
Sunderland Museum and Art Gallery (Tyne and Wear Museums)
Illus. p.30

E.17.	**George Winter** after **Robert William Billings**
Durham from Mountjoy Hill S.E.	1845
Engraving
14.8 x 21.1 cms
Sunderland Museum and Art Gallery (Tyne and Wear Museums)

E.18.	**George Winter** after **Robert William Billings**
Durham Cathedral. The Western Towers from the Windows of the Monks' Library	1844
Engraving and etching
19.9 x 15.4 cms
Sunderland Museum and Art Gallery (Tyne and Wear Museums)
Illus. p. 31

E.19.	**George Winter** after **Robert William Billings**
Durham Cathedral, West View	1846
Engraving and etching, with wash
20.5 x 16.5 cms
Patricia R. Andrew

E.20.	**G. Hawkins** after **John Wilson Carmichael**
Durham, From Framwellgate	1847
Lithograph
11.0 x 16.8 cms
Durham University Library

E.21.	**G. Hawkins** after **W.R. Robinson**
Durham Cathedral and Castle from the North Road
1846
Lithograph
10.2 x 16.3 cms
Durham University Library
Illus. p.32

E.22.	**Frederick Nash**
Durham	1828
Lithograph
16.8 x 25.5 cms
The Dean and Chapter of Durham

F.11. Harold H. Holden
Durham 1927
Watercolour
25.2 x 34.5 cms
Signed and dated
Cheltenham Art Gallery and Museum
Illus. p.37

F.12. Kenneth Steel
Durham No.1
Pen, ink and watercolour
36.8 x 48.3 cms
Borough of Darlington Art Collections

F.13. Thomas Swift Hutton
Durham 1914
Watercolour on board
53.9 x 72.9 cms
Signed and dated
Shipley Art Gallery (Tyne and Wear Museums)

F.14. Leonard Squirrel
A Grey Day in Durham 1939
Watercolour
26.7 x 38.1 cms
E. E. Cleaver OBE

F.15. Byron Dawson
Durham Cathedral 1939
Watercolour and pencil on paper
38.7 x 57.4 cms
Signed and dated
Laing Art Gallery (Tyne and Wear Museums)

F.16. Graham Culverd
Durham Cathedral
Etching
27.5 x 34.0 cms
Victor Watts
Illus. p.38

F.17. Henry Rushbury
City of Durham 1934
Drypoint and etching
24.1 x 32.7 cms
Signed
Sunderland Museum and Art Gallery
(Tyne and Wear Museums)

F.18. Walter Lishman
Durham Cathedral, from Court Lane
Etching
25.0 x 17.3 cms
Signed
Sunderland Museum and Art Gallery
(Tyne and Wear Museums)

F.19. Walter Lishman
Durham 1971
Etching and engraving
21.5 x 30.1 cms
Signed and dated
Sunderland Museum and Art Gallery
(Tyne and Wear Museums)

F.20. Kenneth Rowntree
West Front, Durham 1974
Wood and clay and acrylic on hessian and wood
48.5 x 48.5, depth 2.8 cms
Laing Art Gallery (Tyne and Wear Museums)

F.21. Peter Yates
Durham Cathedral 1976
Thin oil with scumbling on hessian
28.1 x 28.1 cms
Professor and Mrs Kenneth Rowntree
Illus. p. 38

F.22. Dennis Creffield
The South West Towers from the Monks' Garden, the Galilee in the Foreground, Sunset 1988
Charcoal
92.7 x 101.5 cms
The Art Collection, Arthur Andersen
Illus. p. 38

F.23. Birtley Aris
Durham Cathedral: Screen and entrance to choir from the north transept triforium 1990
Watercolour
152.5 x 28.5 cms
Birtley Aris

F.24. Birtley Aris
Durham Cathedral: Bishop Cosin's font cover in the west end of the nave 1991
Watercolour
152.5 x 28.5 cms
Birtley Aris
Illus. p.39

F.25. Eleanor Bowen
Triforium Pulley 1986
Charcoal
42.0 x 61.6 cms
Eleanor Bowen

F.26. Valerie Thornton
Durham Cathedral, Interior 1982
Etching
41.5 x 26.4 cms
Durham County Council

F.27. Valerie Thornton
The Dun Cow 1982
Etching
Irregular shape, maximum 22.0 x 14.0 cms
Hatfield College, University of Durham
Illus. p.39

F.28. **Alyson MacNeill**
Durham Cathedral and Castle
designed for *Kingsgate*, University of Durham
Alumni Magazine, 1991
Wood engraving
Irregular shape, max 4.8 x 12.2 cms
Alyson MacNeill
Illus. title page

F.29. **Hilary Paynter**
Durham   1980
Wood engraving
11.8 x 15.2 cms
Signed and dated
Durham County Council
Illus. p.8

F.30. **Freddy Theys**
Bow Lane, Durham   1990
Etching
34.0 x 12.1 cms
Signed
Patricia R. Andrew

F.31. **Royston Thomas**
Cloisters
Photograph
40.5 x 30.5 cms
Royston Thomas

F.32. **John Erskine**
Romanesque Reflection   1985
Photograph
26.0 x 39.4 cms
John Erskine

F.33. **Angelo Hornak**
Nave Vaulting
Photograph (made for p. 48 of book, *Durham
Cathedral*, text by Debra Shipley, Tauris Parke Books,
1990).
29.5 x 29.5 cms
© Angelo Hornak

F.34. **Angelo Hornak**
Nave from Tower
Photograph(made for p. 104 of book, *Durham
Cathedral*, text by Debra Shipley, Tauris Parke Books,
1990).
29.5 x 29.5 cms
© Angelo Hornak

F.35. **Lindsey McCormick (Ushaw Moor Junior School)**
Flag Design
Crayon and felt-tip pen
28.0 x 60.0 cms
The winning entry to the exhibition's Flag design
competition for the 8's and under

F.36. **Simon Whistler**
Durham Cathedral Goblet
Engraved Glass
25.5 x 10.1 cms
Simon Whistler

F.37. **Fred W. Morgan**
Sketchbook 9   1880
pages 20.5 x 16.1 cms
Royal Institute of British Architects

F.38. **David Gentleman**
Northern Solid Geometry,
page 166 of *David Gentleman's Britain*
Book, pub. Weidenfeld & Nicolson, 1982
Patricia R. Andrew
Illus. p. 40

G.   ARTISTS-IN-RESIDENCE

G.1. **Gerald Davies**
Carving an Icon   1990
Pastel
101.7 x 68.6 cms
Gerald Davies

G.2. **Flick Allen**
Three Figures in Durham Cathedral   1986
Acrylic on paper bonded to canvas
107.0 x 117.0 cms
Private British Collection

G.3. **Virginia Bodman**
Red Column   1987
Oil on canvas
40.7 x 35.5 cms
Virginia Bodman
Illus. p.41

G.4. **Anita Taylor**
Seeking Sanctuary   1988
Oil on card
28.5 x 20.2 cms
Nerys A . Johnson

G.5. **Jo Burns**
Group of Four Cathedral Sketches   1991
Each oil on board
a) *Cathedral from the River Bank 4*
19.0 x 23.0 cms
b) *Cathedral looking West (1)*
19.9 x 24.3 cms
c) *Cathedral looking South East*
21.0 x 27.2 cms
Illus. p.41
d) *View from Prebends with Cobalt 2*
20.5 x 26.6 cms
Durham County Council

G.6. **Matthew Carey**
Candelabra   1986
Charcoal and compressed charcoal on textured
watercolour paper
56.0 x 75.7 cms
Matthew Carey
Illus. p.42

G.7. **Tara Sabharwal**
Magic   1990
20.0 x 25.5 cms
Pen and ink collage
G.I.F. Blacklock

G.8. **Richard Cole**
Durham Cathedral: Interior, South Transept   1993
Etching - artists proof
29.7 x 21.0 cms
Richard Cole

G.9. **Richard Cole**
Tower   1993
Limestone sculpture
44.4 x 12.7 x 70.6 cms
Richard Cole

G.10. **Deborah Gardner**
Guardian Angel   1992
62.0 cms high
Sculpture in ciment fondu
Elizabeth Kessler

G.11. **Colin Wilbourn**
The Last Supper Table   1987
Fumed oak and inlay
Height: 120.0 x 83.0 x 83.0 cms when closed
79.0 x 116.0 x 116.0 cms when open
Colin Wilbourn

H. SYMBOLS AND SIGNS

H.1. **Brancepeth Miners' Lodge Banner**   c1934
Manufacturer, Messrs George Tutill, London
Oil painted roundel set into silk damask
232.0 x 235.0 cms
Beamish, The North of England Open Air Museum
Illus. back cover

H.2. **Agricultural Workers' Banner**   1948
Probably made by Messrs George Tutill, London
Medium/224.8 x 232.5 cms
Beamish, The North of England Open Air Museum
Illus. p.44

H.3. **Fred Taylor**
Durham: It's Quicker by Rail   c1930
Railway Poster
101.8 x 76.3 cms
National Railway Museum, York
Illus. p.43

H.4. **Fred Taylor**
Durham: Cathedral Interior   c1930
Railway Poster
63.7 x 101.8 cms
National Railway Museum, York
Illus. p.43

H.5. **A. F. Kersting**
Durham   1953
Railway poster
79.0 x 58.0 cms
Darlington Railway Centre and Museum
Illus. p.43

H.6. **Edwin Byatt**
Durham Cathedral
Carriage print
15.2 x 41.0 cms
Private British Collection
Illus. p.45

H.7. **John C. Moody**
Durham   1938-9
Carriage print
15.2 x 41.0 cms
Private British Collection
Illus. p.45

H.8. **Sidney Causer**
Durham
Carriage print
15.2 x 41.0 cms
Private British Collection
Illus. p.45

H.9. **Thirteen postcards of Durham Cathedral** (to 1952)

(i) Colour reproduction of painting *Durham Cathedral* by
Maud Fisher
pub. Delittle, Fenwick & Co., York (after 1903)

(ii) 'Pop-up' colour postcard containing small black-and-
white views, *Durham Cathedral, Prebends' Bridge 'We
had a jolly row at Durham'*,
Celesque series, pub. the Photochrome Co. Ltd,
Tunbridge Wells (from 1913)

(iii) Colour reproduction of painting, *Picturesque
Durham: The Cathedral from the Banks*, one of a set of
six by E. Francis, one of Tuck's Oilette Series (pub.
c1910)

(iv) Colour reproduction of painting, *Durham* by
H.B. Wimbush, from one of Tuck's Oilette Series
(issued 1914-1918)
Illus. p. 46

(v) Colour print, *Durham from the Railway Station*, from
a silhouette series by Stewart and Woolf, London,
printed in Bavaria (from 1904)

(vi) Hand-coloured from monochrome photograph, *Durham Cathedral*, from a 'Durham in Winter' series by Valentine and Sons, Scotland (c1905)

(vii) Monochrome photograph of *Durham in Winter* from the 'Auty' series, published in Newcastle, possibly using a photograph of 1899 (from 1903)
Illus. p. 46

(viii) Hand-coloured from monochrome photograph, *The Cathedral - Interior, Durham*, anonymous (posted 1904)

(ix) Hand-coloured from monochrome photograph, *Durham Cathedral Interior*, probably 'Auty' series, printed in Saxony (from 1906)

(x) Photographic reproduction of (?) etching by 'J.C.', *Durham Cathedral from N.*, one of the 'Etchette' series by the Photochrome Company (from 1911)

(xi) Monochrome photograph (with printed blue sky and river area), *Durham Castle and Cathedral*, from the 'Summer Sky' series, Burrows of Cheltenham (from 1905)

(xii) Hand-coloured monochrome photograph, *Durham*, from 'Auty' series (pub. c1906)

(xiii) Monochrome photograph of ink sketch, *Durham Cathedral, North Aisle of Nave*, pub. Photochrome Co. Ltd, Tunbridge Wells (posted 1952)

Collection David Williams

H.l0. **Seven postcards of Durham Cathedral**
(currently on sale in Durham)
Interior and exterior views, all in colour, published by
(i) J. Arthur Dixon
(ii) Judges Postcards
(iii) Format Publications
(iv) Judges Postcards
(v), (vi), (vii) True North Gallery Publications (Mugwump, Durham) - one Illus. p. 46

H.11. **Set of Cathedral Series Postage Stamps**
Issued 28 May 1969
National Postal Museum
Size 2.4 cms x 4.0 cms each
National Postal Museum
Illus. p.47

H.12. **Pitney Bowes**
Durham Postal Franking   1990
2.0 x 4.0 cms
Commissioned by the Dean and Chapter of Durham
Illus. p.47

H.13. **Jonathan Backhouse and Company, Sunderland**
£5 Durham Banknote   c. 1830
Sunderland and Museum and Art Gallery (Tyne & Wear Museums)

H.14. **Josiah Wedgwood & Sons Ltd.**
'Cathedral series' Dessert Plate   1930
Earthenware
Diameter: 22.7 cms
Commissioned by the London and North East Railway Company.
Darlington Railway Centre and Museum
Illus. p.47

H.15. **C. T. Maling & Sons**.
Tea caddy   1929
Blue and white transfer-printed earthenware
Hexagonal, 19.2 x 11.5 cms
Commissioned by Ringtons Ltd. Tea and Coffee Merchants
Ringtons Ltd. Tea and Coffee Merchants

H.16. **Wade Potteries**
Miniature Tea caddy   1989
Blue and white transfer-printed earthenware
Hexagonal 12.8 x 6.5 cms
Commissioned by Ringtons Ltd. Tea and Coffee Merchants
Ringtons Ltd. Tea and Coffee Merchants

H.17. **Mauchline Ware**
Mauchline Ware Glass Holder
Sycamore
Height 8.5 cms; diameter 5 cms at top
John Baker

H.18. **Anchor Company**
Durham Cathedral Embroidery   1940s
Brown cotton thread on cotton base
24.8 x 17.6 cms
Kit embroidery produced by the Anchor Company
1950s: sewn by Mrs M. M. Mackie
Philip and Paula Mackie

H.19. **DURHAM CATHEDRAL - OTHER IMAGES**
(Photographs of items not in exhibition)

a) **Northumbrian Quilting Group**
The Northumbria Quilt   1987
Appliqué, embroidery and Durham Quilting
195.5 x 129.5 cms
Mrs E. A. Trevelyan

b) **Mrs Fellowes**
Sanctuary Ring
Straw, mounted on blue felt and board
48.0 x 35.0 cms
Deposited at the Bowes Museum, Durham County Council

c) **Fred Draper**
Matchstick Model of the Cathedral   1986
Height 93.0, width 72.5, length 199.5 cms
The Dean and Chapter of Durham
Illus. p. 48

e) **Marilyn Hopkins and others**
Sanctuary Knocker 1992
Hooky Rug
Mixed fabrics
91.5 x 122.0 cms
Made by Marilyn Hopkins with members of the public,
in Durham Art Gallery

f) **Royston Thomas**
Feast Window 1981
Colour photograph
30.1 x 20.0 cms
Royston Thomas

g) **County Durham Development Company** 1990
People have always had faith in County Durham
Poster
152.2 x 10.17cms
County Durham Development Company
Illus. p. 47

I.   LOOKING TO THE PAST

I.1.   **Ralph Hedley**
Seeking Sanctuary 1890
Oil on canvas
165.1 x 116.9 cms
Private Australian Collection

I.2.   **Ralph Hedley**
Sketch for Seeking Sanctuary 1890
Oil on canvas
45.8 x 35.4 cms
Laing Art Gallery (Tyne and Wear Museums)

I.3.   **Ralph Hedley**
Seeking Sanctuary
Photogravure
44.2 x 31.5 cms
Julian Brown
Illus. p.49

I.4.   **Alan Sorrell**
Nave of Durham Cathedral
Illustration 22.0 x 17.7 cms from page 17 of book
Norman Britain
text by Henry Lyon
(Lutterworth Press, 1966)

I.5.   **Selwyn S. Beattie**
Construction of Durham Cathedral Roof 1983
Pen and ink on card
60.8 x 52.3 cms
Artist's own collection

I.6.   **Selwyn S. Beattie**
Construction of Durham Cathedral Pillars 1983
Pen and ink on card
63.4 x 52.4 cms
Artist's own collection
Illus. p.51

I.7.   **Selwyn S. Beattie**
*Durham Cathedral as it may have appeared in the
Twelfth Century* 1976
Ink wash on card
48.2 x 70.7 cms
Artist's own collection; used for Durham County
Council's Schools' Pack
Illus. p.51

I.8.   **Thomas William Pattison**
The Building of Durham 1960s
Watercolour
37.8 x 136.8 cms
Durham County Council

I.9.   **Ronald Embleton**
Durham, South West Prospect 1980s
Postcard from painting in bodycolour
15.6 x 21.3 cms
Published by Frank Graham, Newcastle-upon-Tyne
Illus. p.50

I.10. **Ronald Embleton**
*Durham Cathedral, North Side from Framwellgate
c1840* 1980s
Postcard from painting in bodycolour
16.0 x 22.0 cms
Published by Frank Graham, Newcastle upon Tyne
Illus. p. 50

BIBLIOGRAPHY

Books and Catalogues listed here are standard references to each artist or topic. Publications used in the preparation of this exhibition which are not generally available are unlisted, except when they have been used for quotations in the text.

GENERAL

Phyllis M. Benedikz
> *Durham Topographical Prints up to 1800: an annotated bibliography* (Durham, 1968)

Michael Clarke
> *The Tempting Prospect: a social history of English Watercolours* (British Museum Publications, London, 1981)

Howard Colvin
> *A Bibliographical Dictionary of British Architects 1600-1840* (London, 1978)

Marshall Hall
> *The Artists of Northumbria* (2nd.ed., Newcastle, 1982)

Mervyn Holloway,
> *Steel Engravings in Nineteenth Century British Topographical Books* (Holland Press, London, 1977)

Lionel Lambourne and Jean Hamilton
> *British Watercolours in the Victoria and Albert Museum* (Victoria and Albert Museum/Sotheby Parke Bernet, London, 1980)

Douglas Pocock (ed.)
> *Durham Cathedral : A Celebration* (City of Durham Trust, 1993)

Lindsay Stainton
> *Nature into Art: English Landscape Watercolours* (British Museum, 1991)

Tyne and Wear Museums, Exhibition Catalogue by Gill Hedley
> *The Picturesque Tour in Northumberland and Durham, c.1720-1830* (1982)

Grant M. Waters
> *Dictionary of British Artists working 1900-1950*, 2 vols (Eastbourne, 1975)

SECTION A. EARLY IMAGES: THE TOPOGRAPHERS

John Clerk of Eldin
> J. Geoffrey Bertram, exhibition catalogue, *John Clerk of Eldin 1728-1812: Etchings and Drawings* (Edinburgh, 1978)
> Quotation on p.13 from a manuscript in the National Library of Scotland, MS 29.5.7 (iii)

Samuel Hieronymous Grimm
> Rotha Mary Clay, *Samuel Hieronymous Grimm of Burgdorf in Switzerland* (London, 1941)

SECTION B. THE PICTURESQUE

John Sell Cotman
> Miklos Rajnai (ed.), *John Sell Cotman 1782-1842* (Arts Council/Herbert Press, 1982)
> Quotation on p.18 from Lindsay Stainton, *Nature into Art: English Landscape Watercolours* (British Museum, 1991), p.49

Edward Dayes
> [Dayes], *The Works of the Late Edward Dayes Containing Essays on Paintings* (London: Mrs. Dayes, 1805)
> Quotations on pp.15 and 29 are fromDayes, pp. 287 and 255 respectively

Joseph Farington
> *The Diary of Joseph Farington*, ed. Kenneth Garlick, Angus Mackintyre and Kathryn Cave(Paul Mellon Center for Studies in British Art, Yale University, 1978-84)

Thomas Girtin
> T.Girtin and D. Loshak, *The Art of Thomas Girtin* (London, 1954)

J.M.W.Turner
> Andrew Wilton, *The Life and Art of J.M.W. Turner* (London, 1979)

SECTION C. THE GRAND VIEW

George Fennel Robson
> John Lewis Roget, *A History of the 'Old Water-Colour Society' now The Royal Society of Painters in Water Colours* (2 vols, 1891)

John Wilson Carmichael
> Tyne & Wear Museums, Exhibition Catalogue by Andrew Greg, *John Wilson Carmichael 1799-1868; Paintings, watercolours and drawings*

SECTION D. ARCHITECTS AND ANTIQUARIANS

Robert William Billings
> Robert William Billings, *Architectural Illustrations and Description of the Cathedral Church at Durham* (London, 1843)

> Robert William Billings, *Illustrations of the Architectural Antiquities of the County of Durham: ecclesiastical, castellated and domestic* (Durham & London, 1846) and facsimile reprint, Scolar Press, 1974

James Wyatt

James Wyatt's proposals for Durham were researched by R.A. Cordingley, *'Cathedral Innovations'*, in *Transactions of the Ancient Monuments Society*, new series, vol.3, 1955, pp. 31-55.

Colvin's *Dictionary* (under general heading) is the best basic reference for architects of the eighteenth century.

SECTION E. PRINTMAKERS AND TRAVELLERS

Robert William Billings

See Bibliography to Section D.

J.M.W.Turner

Eric Shanes, *Turner's Picturesque Views in England and Wales 1825-1838* (London, 1979)

Exhibition catalogue by Anne Lyles and Diane Perkins, *Colour into Line : Turner and the Art of Engraving* (Tate Gallery, 1989)

Quotation of Turner's instructions to his engravers,p. 30, from W.G. Rawlinson, *The Engraved Work of J.M.W.Turner, R.A.,* 2 vols, (London, 1908 and 1913), from vol.I, p.166

Maps

C. Moreland and D.Bannister, *Antique Maps* (Longman, 1983 and later editions 1986,1989)

Testing the Tourist

D.C.D. Pocock, 'Valued Landscape in Memory: The View from Prebends' Bridge', *Transactions of the Institute of British Geographers*, N.S.7: 354-64 (1982). Quoted pp. 32-33

SECTION F. HISTORIC AND MODERN

Birtley Aris

Birtley Aris, exhibition catalogue, *Durham Cathedral Paintings* (Dean and Chapter of Durham,1990). Quoted on p.39

Dennis Creffield

South Bank Centre, exhibition catalogue, *English Cathedrals: Drawings by Dennis Creffield* (South Bank Centre, 1988). Quoted on p. 38

Kenneth Rowntree

Exhibition Catalogue, *Kenneth Rowntree*, by Michael Nixon, Oriel 31 Gallery, Newtown, Powys, and then on tour, 1991

Leonard Squirrel

Josephine Walpole, *Leonard Squirrel RWS RE* (Antique Collectors Club, 1982)

SECTION G. ARTISTS-IN-RESIDENCE

Durham Art Gallery (formerly DLI Museum & Arts Centre), Catalogues to the Artists-in-Residence exhibitions held at the end of each residency, August-October each year, 1985 to the present.

SECTION H. SIGNS AND SYMBOLS

Mauchline Ware

John Baker, *Mauchline Ware* (Shire Album no.140, 1985)

Trades Union Banners

William A. Moyes, *The Banner Book: a study of the banners of the Lodges of Durham Miners' Association* (Newcastle, 1974)

John Gorman, *Banner Bright: An Illustrated History of Trade Union Banners* (1973, Allen Lane; 2nd edition 1986, Scorpion Publishing)

Railway Posters

Beverley Cole and Richard Durack, *Railway Posters 1923-1947* (National Railway Museum, York)

SECTION I. LOOKING TO THE PAST

Ralph Hedley

John Millard, exhibition catalogue/book, *Ralph Hedley: Tyneside Painter* (Laing Art Gallery, Tyne & Wear Museums, Newcastle upon Tyne, 1990). Quoted p. 49.

Douglas Smith

The Sanctuary at Durham, (Newcastle, 1971)

Brief List of ARTISTS, ARCHITECTS AND ENGRAVERS

See Bibliography for publications by or about individual artists.

Flick Allen (b.1952)
Artist from Cheshire, studied in Exeter and at the Slade, London. Durham Cathedral Artist-in-Residence, 1985-6. Lecturer in art; currently Co-ordinator of the National Association for Gallery Education.
Cat.G.2.

Thomas Allom (1804-1872)
London-born architect, best known for his large output of topographical drawings which were used for engravings. Also a painter.
Cats. E.12 - E.15.

William Angus (1752-1821)
Painter, etcher and engraver, mainly of small topographical bookplates.
Cat. E.5.

Birtley Aris (b.1927)
Born Sunderland, studied in Sunderland and Newcastle. Designed and made stained glass in Newcastle and London; returned to the north-east in 1962. Taught until 1982 and now paints full time.
Cats. F.23, F.24.

Selwyn S. Beattie (b.1937)
Draughtsman, painter in oils and watercolours, and stained glass designer. Trained at King's College, Newcastle. Currently Head of Art and Technology at Greencroft Comprehensive School. Designed exhibits and illustrations for the Cathedral's *Craftsmen for Christ* exhibition.
Cats. I.5 - I.7.

Francis Bedford (fl.1867 d.1904)
Possibly the son of the well-known architect Francis Bedford (1784-1858). Exhibited architectural drawings in London in the 1830s and 1840s.
Cat.D.12.

William Roxby Beverley (c.1811 or 1824-1889)
Also spelt Beverly. Artist, scene-painter, actor and actor-manager, from Surrey. Fluent brushwork in watercolours, influenced by T.P. Bonington.
Cat.F.5.

Robert William Billings (1813-1874)
Architect and author, studied under the topographical draughtsman John Britton and published architectural histories.
Cats. D.4 - D.9, E.17 - E.19, F.4.

Sir Reginald T. Blomfield (1856-1942)
Distinguished architect with a large practice; President of the Royal Institute of British Architects. *Cat.D.15.*

Edward Blore (1789-1879)
Architectural and topographical artist, providing illustrations for numerous books on antiquarian subjects; became a practising architect in the 1820s and was surveyor of Westminster Abbey. *Cats.B.l, B.2.*

Virginia Bodman (b.1954)
Studied painting at Birmingham and the Royal College of Art, London. Scholarship to the British School in Rome, 1981-3. First Durham Cathedral Artist-in Residence, 1984-5. Head of painting at Sunderland University since 1990.
Cat.G.3.

Eleanor Bowen (b.1952)
London-born painter, trained at Camberwell. Now lives in Durham and teaches at the University of Sunderland.
Cat.F.25.

William Brown (fl.early nineteenth century)
Durham drawing master. His son Forster (d.1878) practised as 'penman' at the Mechanic' Institute in Claypath, where he taught **Clement Burlison**.
Cats. E.6, E.7.

Samuel Buck (1696-1779)
Draughtsman and engraver; also an oil painter. Worked with his brother Nathaniel on views of Northumberland and Durham. Best known for the series of Buck's *Antiquities...* (1726-1742).
Cats. A.6, A.9, A.10 .

John Buckler (1770-1851)
Watercolourist, architect and engraver, born on the Isle of Wight, where he worked until 1826. Published engravings of English Cathedrals and exhibited watercolours at the Royal Academy from the 1790s.
Cat.D.3.

Clement Burlison (1803-1899)
Durham artist working on landscapes and portraits, and copies of Italian Old Masters. The Burlison Art Gallery in Durham Town Hall (now the Member's Room) still houses his Bequest.
Cat.F.8.

Jo Burns (b.1959)
Born Sunderland, studied painting in Loughborough and Manchester. Several residencies, including Gateshead Garden Festival, 1990. Durham Cathedral Artist-in-Residence, 1991-92.
Cat.G.5.

Edwin Byatt (1888-1948)
Landscape painter, worked as a commercial and fine artist. Lived in Surrey.
Cat. H.6.

Matthew Carey (b.1957)
Born London, studied painting at St. Martin's School of Art, and Royal College of Art. Lives in London. Durham Cathedral Artist-in-Residence, 1986-87.
Cat. G.6.

John Wilson Carmichael (1799-1868)
Marine, landscape and figure artist from Newcastle; moved to London, then Scarborough. Specialised in north-east views. Large collection of work held at the Laing Art Gallery (Tyne & Wear Museums).
Cats. C.7, C.9, E.20.

John Carter (1748-1817)
Illustrator and engraver of British historical architecture, generally depicting buildings in their original perfect state. Made architectural drawings for the Society of Antiquaries from 1780 and campaigned widely against the destruction of ancient buildings.
Cat. D.2.

Sidney Causer (1876-1958)
Wolverhampton artist who specialised in town scenes and landscapes, often in watercolour.
Cat. H.8.

Ebenezer Challis (fl.1846-1863)
London painter of churches and ruins. Engraved pictures for the Art Journal and other publications.
Cat. E.15.

Frank Chesham (1749-1806)
Draughtsman, etcher, line and aquatint engraver.
Cat. E.3.

John Clerk of Eldin (1728-1812)
From an eminent Scottish cultural family. A notable landscape etcher, chiefly of Scottish views, mainly taken from his own watercolour work.
Cat. A.8.

C. Cole (fl.1801-1810)
Engraver. (Few details recorded).
Cat. E.28.

Richard Cole (b.1952)
Born Rochester, Kent. Studied at Newcastle University; lectured there 1981-86. Artist-in-Schools Project, Gateshead, 1986-87. Works on environmental sculpture. Durham Cathedral Artist-in-Residence, 1992-3.
Cats. G.8, G.9.

Sir J. Ninian Comper (1864-1960)
Architect, born Aberdeen, studied Oxford and London; worked on church restorations and ecclesiastical furnishings and fittings.
Cat. D.14.

John Sell Cotman (1782-1842)
Painter in watercolour and oil, a leading artist of the Norwich school. Born in Norwich, worked in London and his home city. Major collection in Norwich Castle Museum (Norfolk Museums Service).
Cats. B.8, B.9.

Dennis Creffield (b.1931)
London-born artist, studied at the Slade under David Bomberg. Undertook a series of drawings of all the English medieval Cathedrals in 1987.
Cat. F.22.

Graham Culverd
Etcher who worked c 1920s - c 1940s. (No further details traced).
Cat. F.16.

Ian Curry FRIBA, FSA (b.1930)
Cathedral Architect in Durham since 1976.
Cats. D.16, D.17.

William Daniell (1769-1837)
Watercolourist, etcher and oil painter, best known for two collections made from his travels, *Oriental Scenery 1795-1808* 6 vols, (with his uncle Thomas Daniell) and *Voyage around Great Britain 1814-1825* (with Richard Ayrton).
Cat. B.4.

Gerald Davies (b.1957)
Born Wales, trained in Wolverhampton and the Royal College of Art, London. Specialises in drawing. Durham Cathedral Artist-in-Residence, 1988-9. Lives in London.
Cat. G.I.

Byron Dawson (1896-1968)
Newcastle-based painter and draughtsman, specialising in architectural and urban subject matter. The Cathedrals of Newcastle and Durham were favourite subjects.
Cat. F.15.

Edward Dayes (1763-1804)
Now known mainly as a topographer but also a miniaturist. Taught Thomas Girtin and wrote on painting and engraving.
Cats. B.3, E.4, E.5.

John Dobbin (1815-1888)
Born Darlington, a painter of landscapes and topographical scenes; travelled widely but featured north-east subjects in most of his work.
Cat. C.6.

Fred Draper (b.1915)
Lived Sherburn Village, County Durham. Worked in the mines and, later, as an insurance agent.
Cat. H.I9(c).

Frederlck Duncannon, Earl of Bessborough (1758-1844)
Amateur painter and draughtsman.
Cat. E.3.

Ronald Embleton (1930-1987)
London-born illustrator who specialised in 'reconstruction' scenes, especially of Roman life. Lived and worked in Bournemouth.
Cats. I.9, I.10.

John Erskine (b.1947)
Born New Brancepeth, Co. Durham, now lives in Durham City. Works as a Fire Services Officer. Keen photographer with no formal training; has won competitions with the regional NALGO photographic club.
Cat. F.32.

Edward Francis Finden (1791/2-1857)
Engraver of small bookplates; lived and worked in London.
Cat. E.10.

Herbert John Finn (b.1861)
Landscapist in oil and watercolour, and etcher. Studied and lived in London.
Cat.F.9.

Thomas Forster
Eighteenth-century draughtsman and miniaturist.
Cats. A.7, E.27.

Deborah Gardner (b.1963)
Born Newcastle upon Tyne; studied Fine Art at Canterbury and Newcastle. Taught in Australia, 1990-91. Durham Cathedral Artist-in-Residence, 1991-92.
Cat. G.10.

David Gentleman (b.1930)
London based artist, illustrator and designer, who has published several topographical books featuring his own travels and watercolours.
Cat. F.38.

Thomas Girtin (1775-1802)
London born painter who was taught by **Dayes** and studied with **Turner**. Developed the use of watercolour for landscape painting. Influenced by the antiquarian James Moore (1762-1799).
Cat. B.6.

John Glover (1767-1849)
Landscape painter in oil and watercolour. Born in Leicester and worked in London, becoming President of the Old Water-Colour Society in 1815. Moved to Tasmania in 1830.
Cat. B.10.

Moses Griffiths (1749-?1819)
Watercolourist and engraver from North Wales; worked for the antiquary John Pennant and then independently from 1801.
Cat. E.1.

Samuel Hieronymous Grimm (1733-1794)
Born Switzerland, settled in London 1765. Exhibited at the Royal Academy 1769-93. Produced landscapes and topographical drawings and watercolours, and caricatures.
Cats. A.12 - A.18.

James Duffield Harding (1797-1863)
Landscape and topographical painter in watercolour and oils; also an engraver and lithographer. A pioneer for art instruction in schools and a teacher of Ruskin.
Cat. F.1.

Edmund Hastings (1781-1861)
Portrait and landscape painter, working in Durham 1804-1861. Exhibited at the Royal Academy 1804-1827. Sometimes referred to as 'Edward' but 'Edmund' most likely to be correct.
Cats. C.8, F.2, F.3.

G. Hawkins (1809-1852)
Draughtsman and lithographer of architectural and topographical views, working for Day and Sons, London. Specialised in grand, distant town views.
Cats. E.20, E.21.

Ralph Hedley (1848-1913)
Major Tyneside artist; worked in a narrative style depicting north-east subjects, usually contemporary scenes of daily life.
Cats. I.1 - I.3.

Harry T. Hine (1845-1941)
Watercolour painter of landscapes and ecclesiastical buildings. Lived in London.
Cat. F.6.

Harold H. Holden (1885-1977)
Born in Settle, Yorkshire; studied in Yorkshire and London. Principal of Cheltenham School of Art, then Birmingham College of Arts; later the Director of Art Education for Birmingham.
Cat. F.11.

Marilyn Hopkins (b.1950)
Sunderland-born textile artist. Studied in Sunderland, lives in Durham. Has run a series of community projects and workshops in the north-east.
Cat. H.19(e).

Angelo Hornak (b.1946)
Freelance photographer, studied architectural history. Specialises in historic architecture and antiques.
Cats. F.33, F.34.

Thomas Swift Hutton (fl.1865-1935)
Landscape and coastal painter in watercolour. Worked for some years in Cheshire, then in Newcastle; produced several scenes of Durham.
Cat. F.13.

A.F. Kersting
Designer of railway poster 1950s. (No further details traced).
Cat. H.5.

Daniel King (1610-c.1664)
Draughtsman and etcher of architectural views after his own designs and those of his contemporaries. Born in Chester, moved to London in 1656; influenced by W. Hollar.
Cats. A.l - A.4.

John Le Keux (1783-1846) and **John Henry Le Keux** (1812-1896)
Father and son, engravers of small bookplates.
Cats. D.5, D.6, E.9.

William Le Petit (fl. mid nineteenth century)
Line engraver of small bookplates after his contemporaries.
Cat. E.13.

Walter Lishman (b.1903)
Born Stockton-on-Tees, studied at King's College, Newcastle; taught art in Durham. Exhibited widely, particularly in the north east.
Cats. F.18, F.19.

Alyson MacNeill (b.1961)
Scottish printmaker. Studied at Dundee and Glasgow, lives in Brechin. Specialises in wood engraving prints and lino cuts.
Cat. F.28.

Felix Mendlessohn-Bartholdy (1809-1847)
Composer. Toured Britain and visited Durham in 1829.
Cat. B.11.

William Miller (1796-1882)
Edinburgh-born engraver of landscapes and history subject after originals by his contemporaries. Studied in London; lived most of his life in Edinburgh.
Cat. E.16.

John C. Moody (1884-1962)
Painter and etcher of landscapes and architectural subjects. Born at Walton-on-Thames, studied in London and abroad, lived in London and Sussex.
Cat. H.7.

Fred W. Morgan (1860 -?)
Originally an architect's assistant, became a photographer, picture framer and dealer with a business in Durham City in the 1890s. Sketched Durham extensively and published some of his drawings.
Cat. F.37.

James Mynde (fl.1750s and 1760s)
Line engraver of portraits, landscapes and ornithological subjects after his contemporaries. Worked in London, 1740-70.
Cats. A.7, E.27.

Frederick Nash (1782-1856)
London-born architectural draughtsman and lithographer; official draughtsman to the Society of Antiquaries 1807. Praised by Turner as an architectural painter.
Cat.E.22.

Thomas W. Pattison (1894-1983)
Portrait, landscape and animal painter. Taught at King's College School of Art, Newcastle and in Hexham.
Cat. I.8.

Hilary Paynter (b.1943)
Wood engraver and art teacher; currently Hon. Secretary of the Society of Wood Engravers.
Cat. F.29.

John Pearson (1777- ?1813)
Landscape painter from Ripon, who produced a variety of topographical British views.
Cat. B.5.

Robert Pollard (1755-1838)
Etcher and engraver of a variety of subject after his contemporaries. Born Newcastle and apprenticed to a silversmith, moved to London in 1774 and studied painting under Richard Wilson. Set up his own engraving and publishing business in Islington 1781.
Cat. E.8.

Richard Archibald Ray (1884-1968)
Sculptor and painter; born in London but settled in Sunderland, where he was principal of the College of Art and painted many scenes of County Durham.
Cat. F.10.

James C. Redaway (fl. 1830s-1840s)
Line and aquatint engraver of small bookplates after his contemporaries.
Cat. E.12.

Richard Reeve (1780 -?)
Engraver working on a wide variety of subject matter.
Cat. D.3.

W.R. Robinson (fl.1810-1875)
Artist who worked chiefly in Sunderland, though he produced many views of Durham City in the 1840s.
Cats. E.21, F.7.

George Fennel Robson (1788-1833)
Durham Cathedral's most prolific painter. Born in Durham, studied in Durham and then in London, where he became President of the Old Water-Colour Society. Produced an enormous number of paintings, particularly of Durham and the Scottish Highlands.
Cats. C.l - C.5, E.9 - E.11.

Rock and Co.
Engravers and publishers. (No biographical details traced).
Cat. E.23.

J. Roper (fl.1800s)
Engraver. (Few details traced).
Cat. E.28.

Kenneth Rowntree (b.1915)
Born Scarborough, studied in Oxford and at the Slade, London. Lectured at the Royal College of Art, London, 1949-1958; Professor of Fine Art, University of Newcastle, 1959-1980. Lives and works in Corbridge.
Cat. F.20.

Sir Henry Rushbury (1889-1968)
British architectural and topographical etcher and watercolourist from Birmingham; a major figure in etching in the early twentieth century. Official War Artist in both World Wars.
Cat. F.17.

Tara Sabharwal (b.1957)
Born New Delhi, India, studied painting in Baroda and at the Royal College of Art, London. Durham Cathedral Artist-in-Residence, 1988-89. Currently working in New York City.
Cat. G.7.

John Saddler (1813-1892)
Line and mezzotint engraver who produced prints after his contemporaries. Lived and worked in London.
Cats. D.4, D.7, D.8.

Paul Sandby (1730/1-1809)
Like his brother Thomas (1723-1798), a topographical draughtsman mainly employed by the Crown, producing a wide range of watercolours and aquatints of British scenery. Lived in London and worked a great deal at Windsor.
Cat. E.3.

Christof Schwytzer
Seventeenth-century Swiss who produced woodcut book illustrations. (Few details recorded).
Cat. E.25.

Giles Gilbert Scott (1811-1878)
The most eminent Gothic Revival architect of the mid-nineteenth century. Surveyor to Westminster Abbey from 1849. Worked on at least twenty English and Welsh Cathedrals, including Durham in the 1850s and 1860s.
Cat. D.10.

Joseph Clarendon Smith (1778-1810)
Engraver. (Few details traced).
Cat.E.28.

Alan Sorrell (1904-1974)
Painter and draughtsman specialising in 'reconstruction' pictures of archeological sites and historic buildings. Taught drawing at Royal College of Art for many years; lived in Suffolk.
Cat. I.4.

Sparrow (fl. 1775)
Line engraver of small bookplates.
Cat. E.I.

John Speed (1552-1629)
The foremost cartographer of his time, producing a series of County maps of extremely high quality for his publication *The Theatre of the Empire of Great Britain* (1611). Lived in London.
Cat. E.26.

Leonard Squirrel (1893-1979)
Painter and etcher of landscape and architectural subjects, based in Ipswich. Produced several views of Durham.
Cat. F. 14.

Kenneth Steel (1906-1973)
Sheffield-based watercolourist, engraver and lithographer of landscape and architectural views
Cat. F. 12.

James Storer (1781-1853) and **Henry Storer** (1797-1837)
London-based engravers, father and son, working in the mid-eighteenth century
Cat. E .4.

Anita Taylor (b.1961)
Born Cheshire, studied painting at Cheltenham and the Royal College of Art, London. Durham Cathedral Artist-in-Residence, 1987-88. Currently Head of Painting at Cheltenham School of Art.
Cat. G.4.

Fred Taylor (1875-1963)
London artist who produced many art/design posters. Studied at Goldsmith's College. Worked on murals; exhibited at the Royal Academy.
Cats. H.3, H.4.

William Taylor (fl. 1820s)
Line engraver of small bookplates after the work of his contemporaries.
Cat. E.11.

James Edward Terry (fl.1821)
Artist. (No further details traced).
Cat. E.8.

Freddy Theys
Belgian artist living and working near Antwerp. Commissioned in the 1980s by Shotton's of Durham to produce a series of Durham etchings.
Cat. F.30.

Royston Thomas (b.1938)
Durham-based architect turned photographer; has twice won the 'Architectural Photographer of the Year' national title. His work is published in the photographic and architectural press.
Cats. F.31, H.I9(f).

Mark Thompson (1812-1875)
Watercolour painter. (No further details traced).
Cat. D.13.

(?Thomas) Thornton (active London 1778-1785)
Landscape artist and engraver of small bookplates.
Cat. E.2.

Valerie Thornton (1931-1991)
Printmaker who specialised in etchings and engravings of buildings, using rich textural effects. Lived in Essex.
Cats. F.26, F.27.

Joseph Mallord William Turner (1775-1851)
Considered to be Britain's greatest painter. Born London, studied at the Royal Academy Schools from 1789 and enjoyed precocious success. First sketching tour 1792. Worked exclusively as a watercolourist in the topographical tradition to c.1796; turned to oil painting under the influence of Dutch painters and Claude Lorraine.
Cats. B.7, E.16.

Simon Whistler (b.1940)
Glass engraver and professional viola player. Learnt glass engraving from his father Lawrence Whistler. Most work has been executed for commission, mainly in goblet form.
Cat. F.36

Colin Wilbourn (b.1956)
Born Hertfordshire, studied in Newcastle. Several sculpture residencies, currently at St. Peter's Riverside, Sunderland. Teacher Newcastle and Sunderland. Works on projects with Schools and the general public. Durham Cathedral Artist-in-Residence 1986-7.
Cat. G.11.

W. Winkle (fl.l820s)
One of a family of early l9th century engravers.
Cat. E.11

George Winter (fl.1842-1852)
Architectural engraver, based in London.
Cats. E.17 - E.19.

James Wyatt (1747-1813)
Highly influential architect specialising in the Gothic Revival style. Provided designs for controversial 'restorations' at Durham in the 1790s.
Cat. D.l.

Peter Yates (1920-1982)
Architect and artist, exhibition designer and mural painter. Born in London, settled in Newcastle.
Cat. F.21.

E. Young (fl. 1830)
Architectural engraver working in the 1830s.
Cat. E. 14.

LENDERS

John and Anne Abbott
Patricia R. Andrew
Birtley Aris
John Baker
Selwyn S. Beattie
G.I.F. Blacklock
Virginia Bodman
Eleanor Bowen
Julian Brown
Matthew Carey
E.E. Cleaver O.B.E.
Richard Cole
Gerald Davies
John Erskine
Colonel S.J. Furness
Deborah Gardner
Marilyn Hopkins
Nerys A. Johnson
Elizabeth Kessler
Philip and Paula Mackie
Alyson MacNeill
Robert Raymond
Professor and Mrs. Kenneth Rowntree
Royston Thomas
Victor Watts
Simon Whistler
Colin Wilbourn
David Williams

The Art Collection, Arthur Andersen
The Visitors of the Ashmolean Museum, Oxford
Beamish, the North of England Open Air Museum
The British Library
The Trustees of the British Museum
Cheltenham Art Gallery & Museum
Borough of Darlington Art Collections
Darlington Railway Centre and Museum
The Dean and Chapter of Durham
Durham City Council : Burlison Art Gallery, Durham Town Hall
Durham County Council:
        The Bowes Museum
        Darlington Central Library
        Durham Learning Resources
        County Hall
Hatfield College, University of Durham
National Postal Museum, London
National Railway Museum, York
Ringtons Ltd, Tea and Coffee Merchants
Royal Academy of Arts
Royal Institute of British Architects,
        British Architectural Library Drawings Collection
Tyne & Wear Museums:
        Laing Art Gallery, Newcastle upon Tyne
        Sunderland Art Gallery and Museum
        Shipley Art Gallery

University of Durham Library, Palace Green Section
The Board of Trustees of the Victoria and
Albert Museum

In addition, several personal and institutional owners who have lent anonymously .

Photography
Permission to reproduce photographs has kindly been given by:

John and Anne Abbott
Patricia R. Andrew
Birtley Aris
Selwyn S. Beattie
Virginia Bodman
Jo Burns
Matthew Carey
Michael Chase
Richard Cole
Ian Curry
John Erskine
Frank Graham
The Rt. Hon. Viscount Hampden DL
Dennis Hardingham
Marilyn Hopkins
Nerys A. Johnson
Alyson MacNeill
Hilary Paynter
Dr Douglas Pocock
Robert Raymond
Professor & Mrs Kenneth Rowntree
Anita Taylor
Royston Thomas
Elizabeth A. Trevelyan
Victor Watts
David Williams

The Art Collection, Arthur Andersen
The Visitors of the Ashmolean Museum, Oxford
Beamish, the North of England Open Air Museum
Staatsbibliothek Preussicher Kulturbesitz zu Berlin
Bodleian Museum, University of Oxford
The British Library
The Trustees of the British Museum
Cheltenham Art Gallery and Museum
Courtauld Institute of Art, Photographic Survey
Borough of Darlington
Darlington Railway Centre and Museum
The Dean and Chapter of Durham
Durham City Council
Durham County Council
University of Durham Library, Palace Green Section
University of Durham, Alumni Relations Office
Institute of British Geographers
The Mugwump, True North Gallery Publications
National Galleries of Scotland, Edinburgh
National Postal Museum, London
National Railway Museum, York
Norfolk Museums Service
Northumbria Historic Churches Trust
Pitney Bowes plc.
Royal Academy of Arts
Ringtons Ltd, Tea and Coffee Merchants
Tate Gallery Publications
Tyne & Wear Museums
The Whitworth Art Gallery, University of Manchester
School of Architecture, University of Manchester
The Board of the Trustees of the Victoria and Albert Museum

and other anonymous owners and lenders.